C++ for Beginners: Your First Programming Language Explained

Understand Core C++ Concepts with Practical Examples

Eleanor Nash

Table of Contents

INTRODUCTION 5

CHAPTER I: Introduction to C++ and Setting Up Your Environment 6

Why Learn C++? 6

Setting Up Your Environment 11

Understanding the Basic Structure of a C++ Program... 15

CHAPTER II: Fundamentals of C++: Variables, Data Types, and Operators 21

Variables and Data Types 21

Operators and Expressions 26

Type Casting and Constants 31

CHAPTER III: Control Flow: Decision Making and Loops . 38

Conditional Statements 38

Loops in C++ 45

Practical Examples and Mini-Projects 50

CHAPTER IV: Functions and Modular Programming 58

Introduction to Functions 58

Scope and Lifetime of Variables 64

Recursion and Practical Implementations 70

CHAPTER V: Arrays, Pointers, and Dynamic Memory Management 76

Working with Arrays 76

Introduction to Pointers 81

Dynamic Memory Allocation 86

CHAPTER VI: Object-Oriented Programming (OOP) in C++ 93

Classes and Objects 93

Constructors, Destructors, and Inheritance 98

Advanced OOP Concepts 104

CHAPTER VII: File Handling, Error Handling, and Final Project 112

File Handling in C++ 112

Error Handling and Debugging 119

Final Project - A Mini C++ Application 125

CONCLUSION 129

INTRODUCTION

Hi there, and thanks for coming to C++ for Beginners: Your First Programming Language Explained! Whether you are brand new to coding or are switching from another language, this book will lead you through the C++ concepts in an organized and user-friendly manner for beginners.

The sophisticated and flexible programming language C++ is used in the production of high-performance programs, software engineering, and video game development, among other fields. Learning C++ will provide you with a good basis in programming logic and object-oriented design, even if initially it could seem difficult. Though it may first seem challenging, these are abilities relevant to a wide range of languages.

Using this book will help to simplify the C++ learning process. Before diving into more basic concepts like variables, loops, functions, and object-oriented programming, we start with the foundations, which involve defining your coding environment and creating your first program before going on to more advanced topics. Activities, little projects, and real-world examples found in every chapter will help to highlight your learning.

By the time you finish this book, you will be confident enough to create a thorough project applying all you have learned, designing C++ programs, and understanding basic programming ideas. Join me as we go around the universe of C++!

CHAPTER I

Introduction to C++ and Setting Up Your Environment

Why Learn C++?

Among the most potent and flexible programming languages created thus far is C++. Originally developed in the 1980s by Bjarne Stroustrup, C++ has stayed a major player in software development, providing the backbone of many important programs like operating systems, game engines, financial systems, and high-performance apps. Since it offers a strong basis in programming concepts, object-oriented programming (OOP), and low-level system interactions, learning C++ is a great investment for any future programmer. C++ is a necessary language for developers who wish to know how software really runs under the hood since it finds a special balance between high-level and low-level programming, unlike many modern languages that give simplicity over control first priority.

Learning C++ is mostly driven by its efficiency and performance. Being a compiled language, C++ is turned straight into machine code prior to running. This makes it far faster than interpreted languages like Python or JavaScript, which run via an intermediary layer. For performance-critical applications, C++ is a perfect choice since it lets developers directly manage system resources, including memory allocation and deallocation. Where even the tiniest inefficiencies can cause major issues, this degree of control guarantees that C++ is the chosen language for creating high-performance systems, including game engines, real-time simulations, and financial trading platforms.

The great integration of C++ with hardware is another strong argument for learning the language. C++ lets developers' interface directly with system memory, CPU registers, and input/output operations, unlike higher-level languages that abstract hardware details. For operating systems, firmware, and embedded devices— this makes it the perfect language. Because C++ offers fine-grained control over hardware resources, major operating systems, including Windows, macOS, and many components of Linux, are constructed using C++. Learning C++ enables programmers to maximize applications for speed and efficiency in addition to helping them grasp how software interacts with hardware.

Furthermore, a great language for learning basic programming ideas is C++. Because C++ strictly codes and demands students to grasp memory management, data structures, and algorithm efficiency, many colleges and other educational institutions teach programming using it. Unlike dynamically typed languages like Python or JavaScript, C++ calls for explicit data type declarations, which helps programmers grasp type systems more fully. Learning C++ helps novices appreciate more how computers handle memory, run instructions, and process data. Since the ideas acquired in C++ are ubiquitous across the field of software development, this basic knowledge facilitates the transfer to other programming languages.

Learning C++ is also much aided by object-oriented programming (OOP). Among the first programming languages to apply OOP ideas— which comprise encapsulation, inheritance, and polymorphism— was C++. These ideas help developers produce maintainable, modular, reusable code. OOP arranges code into objects that reflect real-world entities, unlike procedural programming, which emphasizes sequences of instructions. This simplifies and scales software development. Learning C++ offers a first-rate introduction to OOP, which facilitates learning of other OOP languages such as Java, C#, and Python. Moreover, many contemporary software development approaches—including design patterns and software architectural ideas— have their roots in OOP ideas with which C++ programmers grow somewhat familiar.

Learning C++ also has the benefit of its great general applicability in many fields. Not limited to one industry, C++ finds application in robotics, artificial intelligence, game development, cybersecurity, and finance technology, among other fields. For example, game creators depend on C++ to create game engines like Unreal Engine, which drives many of the most often-used video games nowadays. The speed and efficiency of the language let game designers create visually spectacular and very responsive experiences. In finance, C++ is utilized to create high-frequency trading algorithms needing microsecond-level execution times. C++ is a fundamental language for robotics and embedded systems since it allows exact hardware component control, hence enabling automation and IoT (Internet of Things) applications. This adaptability guarantees that studying C++ provides access to employment in several sectors.

The great employment market and professional opportunities C++ offers are among its most worthwhile features for learning. From software engineering to systems programming to game development to embedded systems engineering, companies in many different sectors hunt C++ developers for a variety of tasks. Skilled C++ developers are in great demand and command competitive pay since C++ is a rather challenging language to learn when compared to more beginner-friendly languages like Python. Top technological businesses worldwide— including Google, Microsoft, Apple, and Adobe— hire C++ programmers to work on important software infrastructure, including web browsers, compilers, and operating systems. Learning C++ provides programmers access to highly paid and fulfilling employment in sectors of modern technology.

Another great basis for learning other programming languages is found in C++. It fills in between conventional procedural programming and contemporary software development approaches since it blends low-level and high-level programming paradigms. Learning languages like Java, C#, and Swift becomes far simpler if a programmer is competent in C++ since these languages have many syntactic and object-oriented ideas in common. Furthermore, understanding C++ helps one when working with systems programming languages like Rust and Go, which embrace many of C++'s best practices and hence increase parallelism and safety. Starting with C++, programmers have a strong awareness of programming principles, which facilitates the adaptation to other languages and technologies.

The great community and vast ecosystem of C++ are more reasons why learning the language is advantageous. Since C++ has been around for decades, it boasts a large body of libraries, frameworks, and tools meant to simplify development. Among C++'s most useful tools, the Standard Template Library (STL) offers built-in assistance for memory management, algorithms, and data structures. STL lets programmers implement sophisticated features with little effort, hence enhancing code efficiency and productivity. The C++ community is also rather active; open-source projects, forums, tutorials, and documentation easily accessible to students abound. Through websites, including Stack Overflow, GitHub, and C++ forums, experienced coders can assist beginners in learning best practices and troubleshooting problems.

Learning C++ has been vital since its lifetime, and its continuing relevance makes it a language of importance.

For more than forty years, C++ has been a pillar in software development while various programming languages come and go in prominence. In system programming, game creation, and high-performance computing, C++ remains a basic language, even if more recent languages have become increasingly important. While keeping its fundamental efficiency and power, the ongoing development of C++ standards— including C++11, C++14, C++17, and C++20— ensures that the language develops with modern programming needs intact. Learning C++ involves future-proofing one's programming skills as much as it is about picking a valuable ability for the employment market of today.

Learning C++ develops problem-solving abilities useful in any technical discipline, going beyond job possibilities. Masters in C++ gain strong analytical skills since the language demands a thorough awareness of algorithms, memory management, and performance optimization. This ability to solve problems transcends programming and has been used in fields including engineering, data science, and research. Furthermore, extensively used in competition programming, where competitors solve algorithmic tasks under tight time limits, is C++. Learning C++ helps programmers develop their logical thinking and code efficiency, so offering an advantage in coding contests.

Learning C++ is, all things considered, a worthy pursuit for every future programmer. Systems programming and high-performance applications depend on this language since its efficiency, performance, and close integration with hardware define them. Learning other languages in the future will be simpler since C++ also offers a good basis for programming ideas, object-oriented programming, and algorithmic thinking. C++ is still among the most useful languages to learn because of its general applicability across sectors, great job opportunities, and great community support. C++

provides countless chances for development and success, whether your goals are software development, game creation, working on innovative technologies, or improved problem-solving ability.

Setting Up Your Environment

Learning C++ starts with and, most importantly, requires a suitable development environment. Developers must install the necessary tools to set up their systems before writing and running C++ applications. A well-designed environment guarantees flawless coding, debugging, and program execution, therefore removing any setup mistakes and raising production levels. Having the correct tools and a well-configured environment will greatly improve your C++ development experience regardless of your level of expertise as a programmer.

Installing a compiler comes first in building a C++ environment. A compiler is a device that converts C++ source code into machine code, therefore enabling computer operation. C++ calls for explicit compilation before running, unlike interpreted languages like Python or JavaScript. Among the most often used compilers available for C++ are MSVC (Microsoft Visual C++), Clang, and GCC (GNU Compiler Collection). The operating system and the programming development requirements determine the compiler choice. For instance, whilst MSVC is the recommended compiler for Windows-based development, GCC is widely used in Linux and macOS systems. Whatever the decision, effective writing and execution of C++ programs depend on a trustworthy compiler.

Selecting a text editor comes next once the compiler is installed. An Integrated Development Environment (IDE) offers a whole development environment together with project management capabilities, debugging tools, a code editor, and compiler integration. Popular C++ development IDEs are Visual Studio, Code::Blocks, and CLion. Designed by Microsoft, Visual Studio is a strong, feature-rich IDE extensively applied in professional software development. Along with built-in support for version control systems, it offers sophisticated debugging tools and code completion. Conversely, Code::Blocks is a lightweight, open-source IDE with a straightforward, user-friendly design that makes it a great fit for novices. Developed by JetBrains, CLion is a premium IDE with intelligent code analysis, automated refactoring, and flawless CMake, a widely used build system and interface. Although IDEs offer a simplified development experience, some programmers would rather use lightweight text editors such as Visual Studio Code, Sublime Text, or Atom, along with a terminal for building and running applications. Personal inclination and the intricacy of the projects under development determine which IDE or text editor one prefers.

Configuring the development environment comes second once one has chosen an IDE or text editor and a compiler. Setting up environment variables, configuring build tools, and making sure the compiler is appropriately identified by the system constitute part of this. On Windows, developers might have to make the system's PATH variable, including the C++ compiler. This lets the command-line interface easily identify and carry out C++ commands. Usually, GCC is pre-installed or installable via package managers like apt, yum, or brew; Linux and macOS users have. Furthermore, developers who are compiling projects using CMake or Makefiles could have to install and set these tools to expedite the construction process. Appropriate setup of the development environment guarantees that C++ applications may be compiled and run effectively, free from path-related problems or dependence.

Once the surroundings are set up, one must confirm the installation by developing and running a basic C++ application. A simple "Hello, World!" program tests the compiler, IDE, and required setups to make sure they are operating as expected. By means of a test application, possible problems, including erroneous compiler installation, missing dependencies, or misconfigured IDE settings, can occur early on in the setup process. Should mistakes arise during compilation or execution, verifying the environment variables of the system, guaranteeing appropriate installation of the compiler, and reviewing the official documentation for troubleshooting help to fix any setup issues.

Establishing a C++ environment also depends critically on including required libraries and dependencies. Many C++ applications increase capability— such as graphics rendering, networking, or file handling— by depending on other libraries. For instance, although those working on numerical computing may need Boost or Eigen, developers working on game development could have to install libraries like SDL, SFML, or OpenGL. By automatically managing library installations and configurations, package managers, including Conan, ease the process of managing dependencies. Developing sophisticated C++ applications depends on making sure all required libraries are appropriately installed and connected with the compiler.

Furthermore, crucial in establishing a contemporary C++ development environment are version control systems (VCS). Version control lets programmers monitor changes in their code, work with groups, and, should necessary, go back to earlier versions. The most often used version control tool is Git, so integrating it with Bitbucket, GitLab, or GitHub helps to manage projects effectively. Establishing Git in the development environment entails first creating repositories, defining user credentials, and installing Git itself. Many IDEs include built-in Git support, so developers may handle version control straight from the UI. Maintaining a disciplined and orderly codebase depends on knowing how to apply Git commands such as commit, push, pull, and merge.

Another crucial part of a properly designed C++ environment is debugging tools. Having the correct tools helps the debugging process— that is, the identification and correction of code faults. Most IDEs include built-in debuggers that let programmers create breakpoints, examine variables, and walk through code running. Command-line debugging tools, including GDB (GNU Debugger) and LLDB (LLVM Debugger), give a rich understanding of program behaviour. Knowing how to apply debugging tools helps programmers find runtime problems, maximize performance, and raise code quality. By greatly improving the development process, a correctly set debugging environment helps to save time spent on problem-fixing.

Code formatting and style rules are other considerations when building a C++ environment. Keeping a uniform coding style helps code readability and facilitates group projects. ClangFormat and AStyle provide uniformity across projects by automatically formatting C++ code based on preset style requirements. Many IDEs and text editors additionally identify syntactic mistakes, offer code suggestions, and include built-in support for automatic code formatting. Starting with a consistent coding style helps programmers produce professional-quality, maintainable, and clean, easily readable code.

Apart from creating the central development environment, it is equally crucial to maximize the system for enhanced performance. Compiling code can be time-consuming for major C++ projects, yet improving the build process will greatly increase output. Build times can be lowered by accelerating compilation using Ninja and Make, enabling parallel compilation, and optimizing compiler settings. Ensuring the development environment is set up for the best performance guarantees more seamless and effective coding.

Maintaining tools and dependencies currently helps to preserve the C++ environment after it is configured and optimized. Frequent changes to the compiler, IDE, libraries, and debugging tools guarantee conformity with the most recent C++ standards and enhance security and performance. While package managers like vcpkg and Conan make managing library versions simple, many IDEs offer automated updating tools. Maintaining the current ability of the development environment guarantees that developers have access to the most recent C++ features and advancements, therefore avoiding compatibility problems.

To sum up, building a C++ programming environment is a fundamental first step toward understanding and mastery of the language. Essential elements of a good development process are choosing the correct compiler, IDE, or text editor, system setting configuration, library installation, and version control setup. A well-designed environment lets developers concentrate on developing excellent C++ code by facilitating smooth coding, debugging, and program execution. Programmers can increase production, lower mistakes, and produce effective and optimized C++ applications by spending effort in correctly configuring and maintaining the development environment.

Understanding the Basic Structure of a C++ Program

Many contemporary software applications are built on the potent and flexible programming language C++. Any novice must first grasp the basic structure of a C++ program, whether creating basic console apps, sophisticated software systems, or high-performance programs. Every C++ application is developed, compiled, and run according to a set structure that controls. A well-organized program guarantees coding efficiency, maintainability, and clarity.

A C++ program consists of various basic elements, each with a particular use. These elements comprise preprocessor instructions, the primary purpose, comments, expressions, and statements. Knowing how these components go together helps programmers produce functionally coherent and orderly C++ programs. Usually starting with preprocessor directives— special instructions telling the compiler how to handle the code before real compilation starts— a C++ program is structured. Often include header files with necessary capability, including input and output operations, mathematical computation, and file handling; these instructions, Including required header files, allow programmers to access preset features and classes, therefore streamlining the development process and improving program possibilities.

A C++ program has to have a main function per preprocessor instructions. The program's entrance point serves primarily as its principal purpose, so execution begins from this point. Since it specifies the logic to be carried out when the program starts, every C++ application must have precisely one primary purpose. Usually starting with a function declaration, the primary purpose finishes with a return statement, therefore signifying successful program completion. Programmers can create several instructions defining the behaviour of the program within their main purpose. Together, these directions— variable declarations, function calls, loops, and conditional statements— determine how the program runs.

Variations in assignments, function calls, and control structures abound in statements that help to define the logic of the program. An assignment statement, for instance, puts a value in a variable; a function call runs a pre-defined action. Writing functional C++ programs depends on knowing how to use statements properly since they control execution flow and data processing methodologies.

Using comments is yet another crucial component of a C++ application. Though the compiler ignores them, comments— lines of text— offer programmers valuable explanations for reading the code. Comments enable the documentation of the intent of particular code portions, therefore improving the program's readability and maintainability. Comments in C++ can be single-line or multi-line, depending on the length and intricacy of the explanation. Using comments correctly is a solid practice that enhances developer cooperation and code clarity.

Apart from these fundamental elements, a well-organized C++ application usually comprises numerous features. Reusable bits of code and functions assist in dividing a program into smaller, more doable portions and carrying out particular tasks. Programmers can define functions that capture particular capabilities and call these functions as needed rather than writing repeating code. Fundamental to C++ programming, functions enhance modularity, readability, and reusability of codes. Every function includes a body including executable statements, a return type, a name, and, if necessary, parameters. Writing effective and orderly C++ programs requires a grasp of function definition and application.

Important elements of the structure of a C++ program also are variables and data types. A data type tells the sort of data a variable can contain; a variable is a specified memory address with a value. Among the various built-in data types C++ offers are Booleans, characters, floating-point numbers, and integers. Selecting the suitable data type guarantees correct computation and effective use of memory. Variables must be defined before they are used; their values can be changed all through the running of the program. Writing functional C++ programs requires a basic awareness of declaring, initializing, and manipulating variables.

Defining the behaviour of a C++ application depends much on control structures. Conditional statements and loops— which let programs make decisions and run code repeatedly— are among the control structures. Conditional statements— that is, if-else statements— allow a program to run several code blocks depending on particular conditions. Loops— including those for loops and while loops— allow code to run several times until a certain condition is satisfied. Writing dynamic and interactive C++ programs requires mastery of control structures since they let programmers design adaptable and effective logic.

Standard input and output operations are still another crucial feature of the C++ program framework. These processes enable programs to connect with consumers by means of input and output presentation. Usually, standard input and output operations are carried out using the capabilities specified by C++ standard libraries. Programmers can build interactive apps that react to user commands and offer meaningful feedback by including user input and output capabilities. The development of user-friendly C++ programs depends on knowing how to properly manage input and output activities.

Beyond these basic components, object-oriented programming (OOP) ideas could also be included in a well-organized C++ application. As an object-oriented language, C++ supports ideas, including classes and objects. An object is an instance of a class that has data and methods; a class is a blueprint for building things. Encapsulation, inheritance, and polymorphism are OOP ideas that help programmers create scalable, manageable, and reusable code. Organizing a program into classes and objects helps developers construct modular programs with simpler management and extending capability. Mastery of C++ programming and the development of complex software applications depends on an awareness of the foundations of Oop.

A well-organized C++ program also depends critically on error handling. Programs run across unanticipated problems, including file handling problems, division by zero, or invalid user input. Good error management guarantees that software can elegantly identify and fix these mistakes, therefore preventing failures and raising dependability. Exception handling is one of the tools C++ offers that lets programmers properly catch and manage runtime mistakes. Using strong error-handling methods is a best practice that improves C++ application security and stability.

Effective code organization becomes ever more crucial as C++ programs get more sophisticated. Many times, large applications consist of several files with varying application components. Separate source files and header files help to preserve a neat, modular code framework. Source files include function implementations; header files usually include macro definitions, class definitions, and function declarations. Code maintainability, reusability, and compilation efficiency all benefit from this division of worries. Knowing how to create scalable and orderly apps by means of several files helps developers to organize C++ projects.

In essence, any future programmer must grasp the fundamental framework of a C++ application. Key elements of every C++ application include preprocessor instructions, the main purpose, statements, expressions, and comments. Further improving the utility and readability of a program are additional components such as functions, variables, control structures, input/output activities, and object-oriented programming ideas. Mastery of these fundamental ideas will enable programmers to create maintainable, well-structured, efficient C++ projects. Not only does a solid awareness of program structure facilitate coding, but it also provides the knowledge required to address increasingly difficult programming tasks in the future.

CHAPTER II

Fundamentals of C++: Variables, Data Types, and Operators

Variables and Data Types

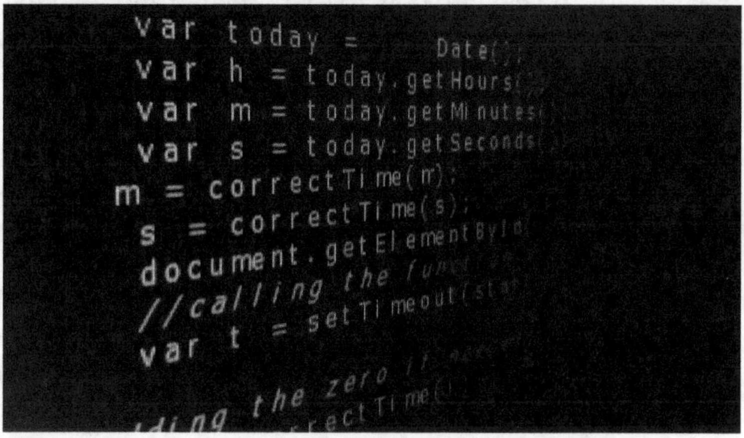

C++ is not an exception; programming languages give a means to effectively store, manipulate, and retrieve data. Using variables and data types— which let programmers define and control data within a program— is one of the basic ideas in C++. Writing useful and effective code depends on an awareness of variables and data types since they define data storage and processing in any C++ application. A program cannot store input, run computations, or retain state throughout running without variables. In the same vein, data types guarantee that the right kind of data is applied in computations, therefore preventing mistakes and raising productivity. Learning the principles of variables and the several kinds of data supported by C++ helps programmers build strong applications to handle data efficiently.

In C++, a variable is a named value-holding computer memory storage place. A variable is termed such since the value kept in it could vary throughout the program running. In C++, every variable has a distinct name called an identifier that lets the program access and work on the kept data. Variable names have particular guidelines to guarantee correct compilation and use. They cannot be a reserved keyword used by the C++ language; they start with a letter or an underscore. Variables should also be meaningful and clear to help to manageable and readable the code. Selecting suitable variable names improves program clarity and facilitates understanding of the code's rationale by other developers.

Apart from name rules, C++ variables have to be declared before they are utilized. Declaring a variable indicates its data type, therefore guiding the compiler on what kind of data the variable will retain. A variable's data type controls the memory allocated for it as well as the kind of operations it can support. Being a statically typed language, C++ requires an explicitly declared data type of a variable at the time of declaration. This guarantees that type-related mistakes at compile-time the compiler may identify, hence producing more dependable and effective code. Maximizing memory use and avoiding inadvertent program behaviour depend on declaring variables with the proper data type.

Several built-in data types available in C++ let developers interact with many sorts of data. Fundamental types, derived types, and user-defined types are the three categories of these data kinds. C++ has as its basic data types integer types, floating-point types, character types, and Boolean kinds. Every one of these kinds has a particular use and a different spectrum of values and memory needs. Whole numbers are stored using integer types; floating-point types handle decimal numbers. Character types save single characters; Boolean types stand for true or false values. Choosing the suitable type for a specific application depends on an awareness of how these data forms interact.

In C++, integer data types span short, int, long, and long subtypes with varying storage capacities. These integer varieties let programmers select the most appropriate type depending on the range of values needed for a project. For situations when just little values are required, for instance, a short integer has a lower range but less memory. Conversely, a long, long integer uses more memory yet has a greater range. Maximizing performance and guaranteeing the effective running of a program depends on selecting the appropriate integer type. Additionally crucial while working with numerical data is whether signed or unsigned integers are required. Whereas unsigned integers are confined to non-negative numbers but give a greater range in the positive spectrum, signed integers can store both positive and negative values. Maximizing available memory can be accomplished by using unsigned integers in cases when negative values are not necessary.

In C++, decimal numbers are stored using floating-point data types. Each of these— float, double, and long double— offers varying degrees of accuracy. Double gives double-precision, therefore more precise for scientific and engineering computations; the float data type offers single-precision floating-point representation. Applications needing very exact numerical computations may find the long double type's even greater accuracy helpful. Many practical uses, including financial computations, physics simulations, and machine learning methods, depend on floating-point values. Still, it's crucial to understand possible floating-point errors brought on by limited precision. When doing arithmetic operations on floating-point values, rounding errors and loss of accuracy can result, so it is quite important to choose the suitable data type and handle floating-point arithmetic properly.

Character data types let C++ apps save individual characters. One character— a letter, a number, a symbol— is represented using the char data type. Every character in the ASCII (American Standard Code for Information Interchange) encoding system is allocated a distinct numerical value. Apart from char, C++ supports the chart type for wide characters and enables the storing of characters from enlarged character sets, including Unicode. Applications needing support for several languages and special symbols especially benefit from this. Many software programs depend on characters since they help to handle text-based input and output and are, therefore, crucial.

Truth values— true or false— are stored in C++ using binary data types. With true corresponding to 1 and false corresponding to 0, the bool data type reflects these values. Conditional statements, loops, and logical operations— where judgments must be made depending on particular conditions— often feature Boolean variables. Programming depends on Boolean logic since it lets one apply decision-making procedures, including verifying if user input is valid or whether a loop should keep running. Effective use of Boolean variables helps programmers to design programs that react dynamically to varying conditions.

Apart from basic data forms, C++ allows derived data types, including arrays, pointers, references, and enumerations. Arrays help programmers manage data collections by letting them store several items of the same data type in a single variable. While references give alternate names for variables, pointers hold memory addresses and offer great power for memory manipulation. These derived data types enable more complicated data structures and memory management approaches as well as improve the performance of C++ applications.

Custom data structures made possible by user-defined data types enhance C++'s powers even more. The definition of complicated data types that aggregate several variables into a single unit depends on the structural and class keywords. While classes provide the foundation of object-oriented programming by enclosing data and action, structures are helpful for presenting related data— such as a person's name, age, and address. Another user-defined type that lets several variables share the same memory space and, hence, maximize memory use in some situations is the union data type. Using user-defined data types helps programmers to produce modular, reusable code, hence improving the maintainability and efficiency of the resulting software.

Another crucial idea connected to C++ variables and data types is type conversion. Oftentimes, one sort of data needs to be converted into another while working with several kinds. Type conversion can be explicit— that is, where the programmer specifies the conversion— or implicit, in which case the compiler automatically transforms a smaller data type to a bigger one. Type promotion, sometimes referred to as implicit conversion, is the process whereby a value is automatically transformed to a suitable data type without loss of information. Explicit conversion, sometimes referred to as type casting, is necessary; nevertheless, when converting a floating-point number to an integer, runs a danger of data loss. Knowing type conversion guarantees that operations involving many data types get the expected outcomes and help prevent inadvertent behaviour.

Working with variables in C++ relies critically on memory management. Effective memory management guarantees the best performance and helps to avoid memory leaks since variables eat memory. Through the new and delete operators, C++ offers dynamic memory allocation, therefore enabling programmers to allocate and deallocate memory as needed. Working with big datasets, dynamic arrays, and sophisticated objects calls specifically for good memory management. Ignoring to release of allocated memory could cause memory leaks, which over time might compromise system performance. Effective memory management allows programmers to produce quick and economical applications using resources.

In essence, C++ programming is built on basic building blocks— variables and data types. While data types specify the sort of data that may be utilized in a program, variables offer a means of storing and manipulating data. Writing dependable and effective code depends on knowing the several data types— integers, floating-point numbers, characters, and Booleans. Furthermore, derived and user-defined data types allow more complicated data structures and object-oriented programming, hence extending the powers of C++. Furthermore, improving the stability and efficiency of C++ programs are appropriate type conversion and memory management. Mastery of these ideas will enable programmers to create strong applications that efficiently handle and process data, hence establishing the basis for advanced programming approaches.

Operators and Expressions

Any programming language— including C++— forms from operators and expressions the basis of it. They let programmers run computations, change data, and control program execution flow. While expressions mix variables, constants, and operators to generate a result, operators are unique symbols that act on variables and values. Writing effective, logical, and functional C++ programs calls for a grasp of operators and expressions. All of these are necessary for creating interactive and dynamic programs, these components help programmers to execute arithmetic operations, compare values, assign data, and make logical decisions.

Arithmetic, relational, logical, bitwise, assignment, and miscellaneous operators are just a few of the various categories into which operators fall in C++. Every category has a certain function and contributes in different ways to programming. Arithmetic operators let mathematical calculations; relational operators compare values; logical operators help with decision-making; bitwise operators work on binary data. While various operators— such as the ternary operator and typecasting operators— offer extra capability— assignment operators save data into variables. Writing simple, succinct code depends on knowing how to use these operators properly.

Among the most often used operators in C++ are arithmetic ones since they are used for fundamental mathematical operations. These comprise modulus operations, addition, subtraction, multiplication, and division. Within their applications, these operators help programmers to handle numerical input and execute calculations. The subtraction operator finds the difference between values; the addition operator lets two numbers be merged. Perform fraction-based computations and scale values using multiplication and division operators. Often utilized in applications including even and odd integers or constructing cyclic patterns, the modulus operator is especially helpful in figuring the remainder of a division operation. Knowing these operators helps one to guarantee correct and quick mathematical computations in C++ applications.

Two values' relationship is found by means of relational operators. These operators consist of equality, inequality, greater than, less than, greater than or equal to, and less than or equal to comparisons. Relational operators employed in expressions produce a Boolean value of either true or false, which lets programmers decide depending on circumstances. Conditional statements, for instance, allow relational operators to verify whether a user's input corresponds with a specified value, whether one number is greater than another, or whether two variables have distinct values. Control structures, including if statements and loops, depend on relational operators since they let a program run various code blocks depending on given conditions. Writing logical and interactive C++ applications calls for a mastery of relational operators.

By letting several criteria be merged in one phrase, logical operators expand the capability of relational operators. OR and NOT are C++'s three primary logical operators. While the OR operator lets an expression be true should at least one condition be satisfied, the AND operator guarantees that several criteria must be true for an expression to be evaluated as true. The NOT operator negates a Boolean value, hence transforming true to false and vice versa. Complicated decision-making processes such as authenticating several user credentials, testing many conditions in loops, and data filtering depending on several criteria often involve logical operators. Understanding logical operators helps programmers create more flexible and forceful conditional statements that improve the interactivity of their applications.

Bitwise operators let programmers operate bit by bit, thereby directly manipulating binary data. These operators comprise AND, OR, XOR, complement, left and right shift operations. Mostly utilized in low-level programming, including system programming, embedded systems, and cryptography applications, are bitwise operators. They permit direct bit manipulation in memory, hence facilitating effective data processing. Bitwise AND, for instance, allows one to extract particular bits from a number; bitwise OR lets one set particular bits to a given value. Optimizing mathematical operations and applying data compression methods depend on the left and right shift operators, allowing data to be moved inside binary representations. For programmers in fields requiring direct hardware interface or memory-efficient computations, bitwise operations are absolutely vital.

Variable storage of values is accomplished with assignment operators. Whereas compound assignment operators do an operation and store the outcome in the same variable, the fundamental assignment operator assigns a value to a variable. These comprise assignments for addition, subtraction, multiplication, division, and modulus operators. Through their reduction of redundancy, compound assignment operators simplify code and increase efficiency. Compound assignment operators let programmers do calculations and assignments in one step rather than writing separate statements. Managing variables and maximizing code execution in C++ applications depend on an awareness of assignment operators.

Apart from fundamental operators, C++ has additional operators that improve functionality. Shorthand for basic conditional expressions, the ternary operator lets an expression evaluate to either one of two values depending on a condition. Working with many kinds of numerical data, typecasting operators help one data type be converted into another. Important in memory management and optimization, the size of operator finds the memory size of a variable or data type. Knowing these little operators helps a programmer to keep readability and yet be able to produce succinct and effective code.

In C++, expressions are combinations of operators, variables, and constants generating a result. Arithmetic expressions, logical expressions, relational expressions, and compound expressions are the several categories into which expressions fall. Mathematical computations form arithmetic expressions; relational expressions compare values; logical expressions assess conditions; compound expressions combine many kinds of expressions. Implementing logic in C++ programs depends on a knowledge of how expressions behave. Assignment statements, control structures, function arguments, and loop conditions all employ expressions; hence, they are naturally part of programming.

The sequence in which operators are assessed in an expression is dictated by operator precedence and associativity. Higher precedence operators— that is, those who are executed first in an expression— have. For instance, unless parentheses are used to supersede the default precedence, multiplication, and division have higher priority than addition and subtraction. Associativity specifies the direction of evaluation for operators of the same precedence. Most operations evaluate from left to right or with left to right associativity. Writing expressions that provide the desired outcomes and prevent logical errors depends on an awareness of operator precedence and associativity.

Expressions frequently feature type conversions when several data types are combined. To prevent data loss, the compiler automatically changes a lower data type to a higher data type in a process also referred to as implicit type conversion or type promotion. Typecasting, or explicit type conversion, calls for the programmer to actively indicate the intended data type conversion. When doing mathematical operations involving several data types, type conversions are crucial since they guarantee compatibility and stop inadvertent behaviour. Knowing type conversions enables C++ programmers to create accurate and effective expressions free of errors.

Another crucial element of creating strong programs is error handling in expressions. Sometimes, expressions have surprising effects such as division by zero, integer overflow, or loss of precision in floating-point computation. Correct error handling methods, including cautious data type selection, exception handling, and input validation, help to prevent runtime problems and increase software stability. Writing statements that consider possible mistakes guarantees that programs operate as intended under several circumstances and give users relevant comments.

All things considered, C++ programming depends on operators and expressions. Operators let programmers do mathematical calculations, value comparisons, logical judgments, binary data manipulation, and variable assignment of values. Forming the foundation of computations and program decision-making, expressions mix variables, constants, and operators to provide meaningful outputs. Knowing many kinds of operators, operator precedence, associativity, type conversions, and error handling guarantees correct and efficient expression writing. By mastering these ideas, programmers may create interactive, strong, optimized C++ apps that efficiently handle and control data.

Type Casting and Constants

Two fundamental ideas in C++ programming that help engineers to properly control data types and guarantee the immutability of values are type casting and constants. The development calls both of these ideas' indispensable. By means of these concepts, one can greatly enhance the flexibility, efficiency, and resilience of code. Understanding type casting helps programmers to operate on variables with a range of data types. Conversely, constants help to preserve the integrity of important data by making it unchangeable during program implementation. This section delves thoroughly into the several kinds of constants and type casting. Described are the several kinds of constants, their uses in C++ programming, and the most efficient approaches to using them.

Type casting— a technique introduced by C++— is sometimes known as type conversion. This method helps one data type to be converted to another. Variables in the computer language C++ are connected to a certain data type, therefore determining the sorts of items they can hold and the operations they can enable on them. On the other hand, there are situations in which the data has to be changed or combined with diverse kinds of factors. Typecasting becomes absolutely necessary at this point. The two main techniques one can apply for type casting in C++ are explicit and implicit casting. Implicit casting, sometimes referred to as type promotion, is the automatic method the compiler does when a smaller data type is transformed into a larger data type to maintain accuracy. Should a variable of type int be assigned a variable of type double, for example, the value of the int variable will be automatically changed to the double value without the programmer's explicit instruction needed. This specific kind of conversion is risk-free since it is quite unlikely that any data will be lost throughout the process.

Most of the time, implicit type casting is able to operate without any issues when there is no chance of data loss during the data type conversion. A smaller integer type, like short, can be raised to a larger integer type, say int or an integer can be raised to a floating-point number (float or double). These are two different kinds of promotions, both feasible ones. Conversely, there are circumstances in which implicit casting might provide unexpected results, including the overflowing of the range of smaller types or the truncation of floating-point numbers. These issues call for explicit typecasting to help to better manage the conversion process.

Type casting, sometimes referred to as type coercion, is the technique whereby a programmer tells the compiler to convert a variable from one type to another. This method is also known as type casting and type coercion. C++ allows explicit casting by use of type conversion operators or functions. These operations force the compiler to treat the data in a specific way, independent of whether or not doing so would cause unexpected results or data loss. When a floating-point number is turned into an integer, for example, the number loses its fractional component. The programmer conducts this truncation on demand to produce the intended outcome. Two main forms of explicit casting accessible in C++ are casting in C-style and casting in C++. In C++, functions including static_cast, dynamic_cast, const_cast, and reinterpret_cast help to accomplish casting. Stating the intended type in parenthesis before the variable, say (int) myFloat, will help one cast in C-style.

The most often used cast in C++ is a static cast. When an explicit conversion between related types is needed, such as when converting from int to float, it is used. Dynamic_cast is used to safely translate references to a class type hierarchy or pointers. This is typically accomplished in polymorphic class hierarchies, in which case runtime validation is absolutely necessary. The const_cast method lets you add or remove the const qualifier from a variable. Reinterpret_cast is a low-level cast allowing conversion between types unrelated to one another. This helps you, for instance, translate a pointer into an integer. Writing clean, efficient, error-free code calls for a strong knowledge of the several kinds of casts and the use cases that are suitable for each of them.

Type casting is used in several programming contexts depending on their need. For example, it could be necessary to cast one or both of the operands to a common type when working with mathematical operations involving different data types to assure compatibility and avoid errors. In C++, explicit casting is usually needed for mathematical operations such as division or multiplication between floating-point numbers and integers. This is taken to maintain the right degree of accuracy. Unless at least one of the operands is explicitly cast to a floating-point type, the result of dividing one integer by another will be truncated to an integer. This holds, but the outcome is shortened to an integer. Conversely, converting a floating-point value to an integer can cause the decimal portion to be truncated. In some cases, including when working with whole number values or designing algorithms that exclusively operate with integer expressions, this could be reasonable.

Type casting is also a quite useful tool when working with functions that accept certain data types as parameters. Designed to take arguments of a specific kind, both the standard library features and the custom functions incorporated in the C++ programming language are the programmer is required to convert the data type of the parameter to the type that is needed in circumstances whereby the type of the argument does not match the signature of the function. For instance, a function needing a double parameter will not work with an integer unless the programmer casts the integer to a double. Furthermore, used is type casting in situations when the size of the variable has to be under control. Type casting is used, for instance, even in memory management and handling binary data.

Though it is helpful, one should use caution while choosing casting forms. Particularly when switching between incompatible types, bugs might be included in a program via casting that is either pointless or erroneous. Should a pointer to a base class type be cast into a pointer to a derived class without dynamic_cast, for instance, behavior that is not declared can follow from this. Along the same line, improper casting between unrelated types with the reinterpret_cast function may cause data corruption and mistakes observed upon memory access. Generally speaking, it is advised to utilize type casting in a restricted capacity and to make sure that it is just done when it is absolutely necessary. Type conversion is required in some cases; it is therefore important to ascertain whether the casting operation is risk-free and does not cause the loss of important information.

Let us now turn our attention to C++'s available constants. Considered constant variables are ones whose values cannot be changed once they have been set. They are a fundamental part of the C++ programming language since they help programmers create immutable values that stay constant while the program is running. When specified values must not be altered to ensure that an algorithm or system behavior is accurate, constants are very useful. For example, C++ applications often show mathematical constants such as the principle of infinity (PI) or physical constants such as the speed of light as constants. This is so since these numbers are constant and need to be kept all through the computer operation.

Constants in the programming language C++ are stated with the const keyword, which comes first then the data type and the variable call. Declared a constant, the value of that constant cannot be changed inside the program for any purpose. Making changes to a constant will cause an error all through the compiling process. This, therefore guarantees the preservation of the integrity of the constant value, so preventing inadvertent modification of important data. Constants are things like item size, configuration parameters, and system-wide values that shouldn't be altered. Many times, constants are employed to explain permanent, unchangeable values. By using constants, which also helps to keep the code simpler and more understandable, magic numbers in the code can be deleted from use.

Furthermore, available in C++ is the constexpr keyword. This keyword is used to define constants that can be assessed throughout the compiling process. Though the compiler guarantees that the value of a constexpr variable will be generated inside the compilation process, the constexpr variable is similar to the const variable except for this. This allows for various optimizations meant to improve program performance. This is so because the value of the constant can be immediately included in the code, therefore removing the requirement for runtime calculations. Creating values used in template metaprogramming, a kind of programming requiring computation occurring during the compilation process, is much aided by constexpr.

In C++, the use of constants goes beyond the limited application of simple data types. Among the various advanced data structures that can be combined with constants are arrays, pointers, and several more. For example, the array might be stated as constant if the size of an array or the components connected with it should not be changed following the initiation procedure. In the same vein, pointers to constant data guarantee that the data being referenced cannot be altered, yet the pointer itself can still be changed to indicate different memory locations. The features of constants discussed here help to enforce strict data integrity and ensure that fundamental values remain unchangeable.

Constants also help to increase the maintainability and readability of code. By substituting meaningful, constant names for hard-coded values, the programmer increases the general code clarity. This helps one to clearly comprehend the value, which helps to simplify the code. In large-scale software systems, this is quite important since the same value might be used in several places. Furthermore, the use of constants helps to reduce the possibility of mistakes since developers are less prone to unintentionally change the value of a constant when the code is changed.

Apart from the fact that they can be used to create representations of fixed values, C++ lets programmers use constants in concert with type casting. To ensure that they match the type expected in a given operation or function, one might expressly cast constants to other data types in sequence. When working with functions that demand specific data types to be used as parameters or when constants are needed to be applied in mathematical processes, this feature is useful.

In C++ object-oriented programming, constants are also quite an important element. The constant keyword can be used all through the class definition process in order to declare member functions as constant functions. It is assured by a constant member function that it will not alter the object's condition. This guarantees that should the function be invoked; the internal data of the object will not be changed in any form. This is quite beneficial when handling immutable objects or using copy constructors that do not influence the original object since it helps to preserve the integrity of the object, which is necessary in some circumstances.

CHAPTER III

Control Flow: Decision Making and Loops

Conditional Statements

Programming is mostly dependent on conditional statements, which also form the basis upon which decisions in the C++ programming language are made. These remarks enable the program to choose among several different execution routes depending on the analysis of the situation. One must be able to add circumstances inside a program if one is to create software that is dynamic and responsive. This helps the software to change with regard to various inputs and circumstances. Conditional statements are distinguished by their capacity to evaluate logical expressions and carry out certain blocks of code depending on whether or not the expressions turn out true or false. Conditional statements are fundamentally these. Those learning C++

programming certainly must have a strong grasp of how to effectively employ conditional statements.

Conversely, if, else, and else if statements, as well as the switch statement, provide all instances of conditional statements applicable in C++. By use of these assertions, programmers may control the flow of execution, design complex decision-making procedures, and ensure that the program responds appropriately in a range of circumstances. Every one of these remarks has a different purpose; hence, it is essential to have a strong grasp of their syntax and behaviour if one wants to create not just functional but also clear and effective code.

The most basic conditional statement available in C++, the if statement, is the foundation for most of the language-supported decision-making processes. The if statement evaluates a condition— a Boolean expression— by means of which a block of code is only executed should the evaluation of the condition prove to be true. Should the condition prove to be false before the program evaluates, it will avoid the part of code linked with the if expression. This is often taken into account in situations when a given activity should only be engaged under particular circumstances. An if statement could be used, for example, to ascertain whether or not a given number is positive or negative, therefore helping to ascertain whether the user's input meets particular criteria. Because it is so simple, the if statement is a must-have tool for programmers' toolkit.

When used in its most basic form, the if statement is preceded by a condition encapsulated in parenthesis. Should the condition be met, the code housed within the block after the if statement is executed. Should the condition fail, the program will proceed to the next part of the code situated outside the if block. On applications used in the real world, however, a single condition is usually inadequate to characterize the behaviour of the program. C++ features the else statement to handle circumstances like these. This line of code allows programmers to offer a backup block should the condition mentioned in the if statement be improperly assessed.

Using the otherwise statement in combination with the if statement is standard procedure to indicate another way of action for the computation. Should the condition within the if statement prove to be false, the program moves to the block of code following the else statement. This is useful in situations where one action is needed when a condition is satisfied, but another action is needed to the same degree when the condition is not satisfied. One may use an if-then structure, for example, to ascertain whether or not a user has entered a valid password. Should the password be erroneous, an error notice could show up to the user; should the password be correct, the software might move forward into the next phase of operations.

Many times, it is required to assess several circumstances in their separate sequences. The programming language C++ features an else if statement that allows one to examine numerous conditions in a sequential manner, therefore overcoming this problem. This is the scenario in which the else if statement is useful: the computer must choose one of the several alternative blocks of code to use since several elements are incompatible with each other. The software looks at the state of the condition in the else if statement when the if condition proves to be false. Should this condition be satisfied, the connected code block to the else if expression will run. Should the condition contained inside the else if statement proves to be untrue, the program can either go to the last else block should none of the other else if conditions be found to be satisfied or keep checking other else if conditions.

Using the else-if statement helps one choose from various possibilities when faced with them. For example, an application could be needed to investigate the value of a variable and do different actions depending on whether or not the value fits one of several ranges. Without the else if statement, nested if-else statements would be used instead, which could make the code less clear and more difficult to maintain and implement. Apart from that, the else if structure helps the programmer to understand this process and lets him create more compact and simple code. Only one block of code runs in an if-else if-else chain; this block of code is decided by the first condition that finds truth. One should pay great attention to this point. Once a real condition has been found, the other conditions are thrown off and ignored.

Although the if-else and else-if statements allow for flexibility, there are situations when it is required to verify several conditions at once. One can reach this aim by using logical operators such as && (AND), OR, and! (NOT). Logical operators let one integrate several criteria into a single statement, therefore facilitating more difficult decision-making circumstances. One condition that might be employed is one that makes use of the && operator to ascertain whether or not a variable fall between zero and less than ten. Like in the past example, one can find whether a variable is either less than zero or greater than ten by means of the || operator. Negating a condition using the! Operator helps one to ascertain whether a condition is false.

Using logical operators in combination with conditional expressions raises the capacity of decision-making within C++ applications. If programmers combine various events into one phrase, they can create more complicated reasoning without using separate if-else blocks. Thanks to the logical operators, which increase the program's usability and responsiveness, C++ applications are able to make subtle judgments depending on a range of circumstances. However, logical operators should be used sparingly as, if used too often, complicated circumstances can become difficult to understand and keep up with.

Though effective tools for decision-making, if, else, and else if statements can often be challenging when there are numerous different situations to consider. This is so since they are employed for a set of criterion reviews. In circumstances such as these, the switch statement could be a great fit. One expression can be assessed against several alternative values by means of the switch statement. The switch statement is used to streamline the process of creating code that must select among a great number of options depending on the value of a single variable.

The expression is assessed and its value is matched with several case labels such that the switch statement runs as intended. The code that corresponds with one of the case labels is executed successfully whenever the value of the expression is discovered to be exactly matching. The switch statement is a better approach than a series of if-else if statements in managing numerous situations. This is especially true in cases when the basis of the conditions is the value of one variable. After a case match ends, the program will keep running until it finds a break statement, which will cause the switch block to be stopped. Should no case matching be discovered, the designated default block will be followed. The default block offers a fallback wherein the program will continue to operate in a predefined way even in the case that none of the specified conditions are satisfied.

Usually producing code that is simpler to understand and maintain than a succession of if-else lines, the switch statement Using the switch statement is clearly one of the most important benefits. Using a switch statement may let a program run several codes depending on the value of an integer or an enumeration, for example, be more understandable and simpler. This is so because the switch statement lets the machine run several codes. This is especially true in cases when one has to examine several possible values. Switch statements do have certain limits, though. One of these drawbacks is their incapacity to evaluate intricate conditions or phrases devoid of equality. Still, for situations that are far more complicated, if-else statements should be applied.

When working with conditional expressions in the C++ programming language, careful thought of the flow of execution is important. Not only are nested if-else statements robust, but if they are not set up correctly, they could soon get challenging. Deeply nested conditionals in a code can make debugging, reading, and maintaining more challenging. Many times, early returns in order to simplify the flow of execution or restructure the code into smaller functions that are simpler to maintain or utilize are better options than either approach. By using a clear and straightforward approach to conditional logic, developers may create less prone to error but also simpler to understand codes.

Using conditional expressions still brings performance into another important issue. In some cases, especially when several conditions need to be considered, complex conditional logic might affect the efficiency of a program. For instance, the use of logical operators in concert with several conditions could cut the execution time. This is particularly true in cases where the conditions ask for expensive computations or function calls. Reducing the number of scenarios that need to be investigated and ensuring that the ones most likely to arise are verified first will help to maximize conditional logic. When the conditions are mostly predictable, it could be helpful to reorganize them such that the number of irrelevant comparisons is reduced.

Conditional statements are also rather crucial in the management of mistakes and exceptions in C++

systems. Many applications involve circumstances whereby specific requirements must be met for the program to run in the proper course. Should these requirements not be met, the program should start remedial action. Usually, this is achieved by means of conditional statements, which are used to verify mistakes, including erroneous user input, failed file operations, or unanticipated system activity. A program that employs an if statement to ascertain whether or not a file already exists before trying to open it would be one instance of this. In the same vein, a program might manage several types of user input with an if-else block. This ensures, then, that, in extraordinary conditions, the program won't become unresponsive or produce erroneous results.

Conditional statements are, all things considered, a necessary feature of the C++ programming language since they enable developers to create dynamically responsive applications. The if, else, else if, and switch statements let one run several blocks of code depending on the outcome and assess conditions in several ways. It is imperative to have a strong awareness of how to properly use these ideas in order to generate code that is functional, efficient, and maintainable. By using conditional statements in combination with logical operators and carefully controlling the flow of execution, programmers are able to build sophisticated decision-making systems that can intelligibly react to changing inputs and conditions. Moreover, the process of correcting mistakes and ensuring the durability of a program depends on conditional expressions absolutely. A good C++ programmer must first master conditional statements if he is to advance. This is valid whether you are creating complex systems or simple apps.

Loops in C++

A basic tool in programming, loops let a block of code be repeatedly executed, hence automating chores that would otherwise call for human repetition. Loops give a quick approach in C++ to run a sequence of instructions several times under specified criteria. Using loops helps programmers maximize their code to manage repetitious jobs with little effort, therefore increasing productivity and lowering the possibility of mistakes. For iterating over data, manipulating vast amounts of information, and controlling repeated calculations, loops are vital tools. The several forms of loops in C++, their syntax, their functionality, and recommended practices for efficient loop use in C++ programming are investigated in this section.

Fundamentally, C++ loops let the computer run a set of instructions until a specific condition is satisfied. In C++, the main loop varieties are the do-while, while, and for loops. Every one of these loop forms has a somewhat different function and finds particular application in particular contexts. Create legible and effective C++ code by knowing when and how to apply these several loop structures.

Among the most often used loop structures in C++ are ones of for loops. It is mostly employed in cases when one knows the number of iterations ahead of time. The for loop is made to operate per pre-iteration evaluated criteria. Three sections make up its structure: the condition, the initialization, and the increment or decrement. The increment or decrement changes the loop variable following each iteration; the condition is assessed prior to each iteration to ascertain if the loop should be kept running. For iterating across arrays, doing a certain number of calculations, or managing repeated operations with a predefined endpoint, the for loop offers a neat approach to convey loops with a well-defined number of iterations.

The for loop's clear syntax and simplicity help to be among its main benefits. The loop header contains all three elements of the loop: initializing, condition, and increment, so the programmer may quickly grasp the behaviour of the loop. When iteratively over sequences, such as arrays or containers in the Standard Template Library (STL), the for loop is especially helpful. For instance, the for loop offers a quick and easy way for you to iterate over the contents of an array and execute a computation on every element.

Conversely, the while loop runs as long as a certain condition is true, but the number of repetitions is unknown ahead of time. Before every iteration, the while loop assesses the condition; if the condition is true, the block of code housed inside the loop runs. When the termination condition depends on elements decided upon during the loop's execution, the while loop is very helpful. A while loop can be used, for instance, to process user input, search for specified circumstances, or repeat a chore until a designated event happens.

The while loop lacks an initialization or increment in the loop header, unlike the for loop. These acts have to be managed independently inside the loop body. Consequently, the while loop is more flexible than the for loop but calls for more careful control of the beginning and update processes of the loop. Using a while loop might cause infinite loops if one forgets to change the loop variable. Ensuring that the condition of the loop is eventually assessed as false and that the loop variable is changed suitably inside the loop body helps to prevent this.

Though it guarantees that the block of code inside the loop will be performed at least once, the do-while loop is identical to the while loop except for one critical distinction. This is so because, instead of preceding it, the do-while loop tests the condition following every iteration. Consequently, even in cases when the condition is false on the first assessment, the loop will always run its body at least once. When the code inside the loop has to be run at least once before evaluating the condition, the do-while loop is handy. Menu-driven systems, for instance, need the user to select an option, so the menu must be shown at least once before the condition is checked to ascertain whether the user wants to proceed.

The structure of the do-while loop is a do block followed by the loop body; the condition is tested following block execution. Should the condition be such, the loop keeps running. Should it prove untrue, the loop ends. This kind of loop is perfect when the first action ought to be carried out before the condition is assessed. To stop infinite loops, nevertheless, care must be made to guarantee that the loop condition is accurately updated inside the loop body, just as in the while loop.

Although the most often used loop structures in C++ are the for, while, and do-while loops, it is crucial to know their respective suitable use cases and variations from them, the particular work being done determines mostly the loop to be used. While the while loop is more suitable for situations where the termination condition of the loop is based on runtime criteria, the for loop is best suited for circumstances where the number of iterations is known in advance. When the body of the loop must be running at least once before assessing the state, the do-while loop is perfect.

Beyond the fundamental loop structures, C++ offers control methods such as break and continue that enable more freedom and control over the running of the loop. Whether or not the termination condition of the loop has been satisfied, the break statement allows one to leave a loop early. Conversely, the continuous statement lets the program bypass the remaining code in the current iteration and advance to the next one of the loops. In complicated loop situations— where some conditions can call for an early departure or a skip to the next iteration— both of these control statements can be useful.

When a loop is looking for a specific value or condition, and once it is located, the loop can be stopped with a break statement most of the time. The break statement can be used, for instance, to stop a loop iterating through an array in search of a certain integer, therefore stopping wasteful iterations. In loops, too, the continue statement can be used in cases whereby the program must skip the current iteration based on certain criteria. A loop processing a list of numbers, for instance, might only go over positive numbers while skipping over negative values.

Another important factor is loop performance, particularly in relation to computationally demanding activities like big data processing. Although loops are great tools for automating repeated chores, improperly written loops can cause inefficiencies and performance issues. Reducing the work completed inside the loop body helps to enhance loop performance. For a loop doing costly calculations or I/O operations, for example, it could be feasible to rework the code to cut the frequency of these operations.

Another crucial performance factor is loop unrolling, a method meant to boost loop efficiency by lowering iteration count. This can especially help in tight loops where the overhead of assessing the loop situation and changing the loop variable can be somewhat important. In loop unrolling, one manually increases the number of operations carried out each iteration to lower the total number of iterations. This method should be applied carefully, though, since it could complicate the code and complicate maintenance of it.

Apart from efficiency, one should take the readability and maintainability of loops into great importance. Although loops are great tools, if they are excessively complicated or highly nested, they can also become challenging to grasp. Using descriptive variable names, keeping the loop body compact, and avoiding too much nesting help to keep readability intact. Breaking the code into smaller functions or refactoring the logic into simpler stages could help when loops grow overly complicated.

Additionally, very important in error handling and exception management are loops. In cases when input is handled inside a loop, for instance, it could be required to validate the input and manage mistakes correctly. Should invalid input be found, the loop can ask the user for fresh input or skip the invalid item and carry on processing the remaining data. Similarly, loops can be used to retry actions that might fail intermittently, such as network requests or database operations, thereby guaranteeing that the program stays strong and fault-tolerant.

In C++, loops also find application in repeated operations-requiring algorithms such as sorting and searching ones. To compare and reorder elements in a collection, for instance, bubble sort or quicksort mostly depend on loops. Likewise, loops are used in search algorithms— linear or binary— to examine data and find certain elements. Many applications depend on these basic algorithms, which also rely on loops to effectively analyse large amounts of data.

In games and simulations, where they are used to continually change the game state or replicate the passing of time, loops are also vital. Loops in these uses repeatedly run code updating the game environment, search for user input, and generate images, therefore regulating the flow of the program. Usually running constantly until a termination condition— such as the user quitting the game or running out of the simulation—game loops run.

In essence, loops are a fundamental feature of C++ programming that allows code to be repeatedly executed depending on particular criteria. Although each for, while, and do-while loops have special advantages and applications, knowing when and how to apply them is crucial for producing competent and productive code. Loops offer strong instruments for program flow control, data processing, and automation of repeated chores. Designing loops calls for careful balancing of performance with readability and maintainability. Effective use of loops helps programmers to handle challenging tasks, increase program efficiency, and provide more dynamic and responsive applications.

Practical Examples and Mini-Projects

Regarding learning and mastering any programming language, including C++, real-world projects and smaller tasks are rather important. Although theoretical knowledge and a grasp of syntax constitute the basis of programming ability, it is the practical application of this knowledge that helps developers to properly understand the concepts and discover answers to difficulties arising in the real world. Not only are the ideas reinforced, but also the learners are exposed to the problems and problem-solving elements that are intrinsically related to software development by using the abilities acquired through practical coding and project development in C++. Working through real-world examples and small projects will help beginners increase their knowledge, confidence, and position to handle more advanced programming assignments.

Practical experience is absolutely necessary for one to have a deeper awareness of C++ during the learning process. Practical examples help to clarify the application of numerous programming components in order to address challenges more complex than simple exercises. Among these constructions are variables, data types, control flow, loops, and functions. These examples help the students to link the abstract ideas they have studied with the practical process of developing, debugging, and code testing. This approach helps to close the difference between theoretical knowledge and its implementation in the real world. The usefulness of practical examples and mini-projects in the study of C++, their part in the development of skills, and the manner in which they can equip programmers for more difficult software engineering chores will be discussed in this section.

One of the first useful cases one might find in the C++ programming language is working with fundamental input and output, the basis of interactive programs. For example, building a basic calculator application is a great exercise for novices since it will help one learn how to manage user input, perform arithmetic operations, and output results. By means of this simple project, students have the chance to acquire knowledge in using conditional expressions (such as if, otherwise if, and then), loops for executing repeated activities, and functions for obtaining modularity in their code. Students learn how to handle user input, how to process different kinds of data, and how to produce output in an organized way by use of a calculator under development. By means of tasks of this kind, students can improve their aptitude for logical reasoning and problem-solving— qualities needed for more challenging programming operations.

Students will be able to handle more challenging projects that fully use the C++ programming language as they develop in their studies. One project that shows the creation of random numbers and simultaneously reinforces control flow structures is the building of a number guessing game. The computer software will generate a random number for this mini-project, and the user will be challenged to try to guess the number inside a given range. The application may provide comments on whether the prediction is too high or too low; the program will run until the right amount is projected. This project teaches the idea of game logic, which is a necessary component in the process of building interactive applications; it also combines basic concepts, including loops, conditionals, and input validation. Including other elements, such as a counter for the number of attempts, varying difficulty levels, or a timer, will help Mini-projects like this to be even better. This will inspire students to give their programs more thought for expansion and improvement.

One of the most important benefits of practical projects is that they force students to consider edge cases and control exceptions while they are working on them. In the game of number guessing, for example, it is quite crucial to ensure sure the user enters appropriate numerical inputs and to control circumstances whereby the input is either non-numerical or outside of the range. By means of this idea, students are guided in understanding the need for input validation and exception management. These are the fundamental abilities needed for the evolution of robust software. Learners should grow at ease using strategies like try-catch blocks to handle likely exceptions and create logic guiding the user to provide appropriate input. A vital part of software development, error management should be familiar to students.

Students will get the chance to engage in projects including file input and output (I/O), which is a skill necessary for working with data derived from the practical world as they create ever more complex programs. Under this framework, one may classify the creation of a contact management system as a simple mini-project. Students would be expected to create a program for this project whereby the user may see, add, remove, and change contacts from a file. The system might save the person's contact data— name, phone number, and email address— in a text file. By means of examples, this project guides students in handling files in C++, including reading from and writing to files. Furthermore, it allows users to work with dynamic memory allocation and pointers— two ideas important for the efficient management of data in more extensive systems. These kinds of projects give students the chance to learn about real-world problems, including maintaining data durability and assuring data integrity, both of which are fundamental requirements of creating software systems.

Still, another field where practical examples and mini-projects shine is the development of simple video games. Making a text-based replica of a popular game is one of the most common tasks for students who want to raise their C++ programming ability. Among such games are Tic-Tac-Toe and Hangman ones. Among the more advanced concepts these simulations introduce are arrays, multidimensional arrays, and two-dimensional data structures. For instance, the game board of Tic-Tac-Toe is usually shown as a three-by-three array. This forces the program to track player movement positions, ascertain whether the player satisfies the winning criteria, and display the revised board following every action. The creation of such a game depends on careful control of game states, conditionals, loops, and input validation in turn. By means of these kinds of projects, students not only have the chance to apply the basic concepts of C++ but also acquire knowledge of the structure of games and interactive apps, thus providing the framework for more advanced game development tasks.

Should one be inclined to work on more complex projects, one could try to create a basic text editor or a to-do list application. While a to-do list app might let users add, delete, and view tasks, a text editor might let users create, change, and save text content. For users, both of these characteristics are helpful. To use these apps, students must grasp the use of functions, data structures such as arrays or vectors, file input and output, and maybe object-oriented programming (OOP) concepts such as classes and objects. Students will experience problems related to the management of user input, the guarantee of data permanency, and the use of a responsive interface during the development of these apps. By using these projects, students can develop a more thorough understanding of how to plan a program, manage resources, and guarantee that their code is both maintainable and scalable.

Completing mini-projects using object-oriented programming (OOP) will help the learner to better grasp C++'s advanced features. One simple object-oriented programming (OOP) effort may be designing a "Bank Account" class. Students in this session would be able to develop skills including account number, balance, depositing, withdrawing, and checking techniques. Over the course of this project, students learn classes, constructors, destructors, and member functions, among other ideas. Apart from this, it emphasizes the need to develop modular and reusable building codes as well as one of the four fundamental ideas of object-oriented programming (OOP), encapsulation, together with inheritance, polymorphism, and abstraction. Through building such object-oriented programming (OOP)--based mini-projects, students gain a fundamental knowledge of how to organize intricate systems and apply C++ to generate maintainable software.

Working on mini-projects requiring the use of libraries and outside frameworks allows students to gain actual expertise with the resources at hand, thereby arming developers. By means of a mini-project utilizing the C++ Standard Template Library (STL), students can acquire expertise in handling a number of data structures, including vectors, stacks, and queues, as well as algorithms, such as sorting and searching. Using STL not only saves time but also teaches students how to include previously thoroughly proven code in their projects. Furthermore, students can be exposed to visual programming and game development using outside libraries like SFML or SDL for the aim of creating basic graphical apps like games. Anyone who wants to create a game or GUI (graphical user interface) utilizing the C++ programming language can find great advantages from this exposure.

One of the challenges related to practical examples and mini-projects is that they may quickly get more complex as the project's scope grows. Students could struggle with huge data management, code organization, concurrency multi-threading, or other areas. Students might face these difficulties. Building a basic application for a to-do list, for example, could seem like a simple chore at first, but once students add extra features— such as the ability to sort tasks, due dates, or reminders— they will meet complexity more closely reflecting the real world. Students learn the skills required to create clean, modular, modular code, make efficient use of debugging tools, and follow the best standards as they work through these challenges. Students get the chance to acquire the necessary capacity for developers— that of managing complexity. Working on increasingly difficult undertakings will help one to grow in this capacity.

Another absolutely important lesson learned from working on actual cases and small projects is the need for testing and debugging. Once a piece of code has been developed, thorough testing on it is absolutely essential to ensure it runs as expected. All potential actions in this regard are using unit tests to make sure every component of the software is operating as it should and debugging the program upon errors. Debugging helps students to learn logical analysis of their code, identification of issues, and effective resolution of them. Many programmers in C++ see debugging as among the most useful abilities they might pick up. Mini-projects are so popular since they offer a perfect chance to exercise this talent in a regulated environment.

Not least of all, the mini-project and practical example completion process gives students the chance to create a portfolio of their work. Having a portfolio of completed projects can be quite helpful whether one is searching for employment or developing a programming career. It is proof that a student can apply their knowledge to problems that arise in the actual world, practice critical thinking, and overcome challenges. Furthermore, the creation of a portfolio comprising several projects shows a learner's development over time, starting with simple tasks and moving to more advanced uses. This shows the students' will to become C++ masters.

Regarding learning C++, it is imperative to have both mini-projects and real-world examples to go through. Apart from offering a practical, hands-on approach to acquiring programming concepts, they also help to validate the knowledge acquired by means of theoretical study. When students utilize coding to tackle problems directly relevant to the real world, they enhance their problem-solving skills, boost their confidence in their programming ability, and prepare for ever challenging assignments. Mini-projects let students put their knowledge to use in relevant and useful contexts. From the building of simple calculators and games to more sophisticated applications involving file handling, object-oriented programming, and outside libraries, these mini-projects can span everything. Completing these projects imparts important vital abilities required for professional software developers to succeed. These skills cover program management, testing, and debugging, thereby addressing complexity. Ultimately, the most crucial component in developing mastery of C++ and learning the skills required to generate software capable of being durable, efficient, and scalable is acquiring practical experience by means of the completion of mini-projects.

CHAPTER IV

Functions and Modular Programming

Introduction to Functions

One of the basic building blocks of C++ programming, functions provide a means for code organization, hence enhancing its reusability and readability. In programming, a function is a self-contained code unit meant for a particular use. Functions help a programmer to specify a series of instructions that may be carried out upon demand, therefore streamlining the general design and development of projects. Divining a program into reasonable portions helps functions support modularity, organization, and better structure. Writing clear, efficient, and maintainable code in C++ depends on functions absolutely. By dissecting issues into smaller, more doable chores, they enable their resolution. Anyone learning C++ must first grasp the fundamental ideas of functions, their syntax, and their part in the language. The idea of functions in C++ will be discussed in this section, together with its forms, syntax, benefits, and ways in which they help a program to be functional.

Although all programming languages include the universal idea of functions, C++ adds some special characteristics that provide functions with specific relevance. Functions in C++ let developers create reusable code sections accessible from many areas of a project. By letting the same code be used across several sites, functions not only improve code structure but also help to lower redundancy. This can help to greatly lower mistakes, simplify the code, and improve its readability.

Usually consisting of many important components— the return type, the function name, the parameter list, and the body of the function—are C++ functions. The return type specifies, if any, the kind of value the function will produce following its running through. A function might, for example, produce an integer, a float, a text, or perhaps a bespoke data type before the function name becomes the return type. The function name is a special identification used to invoke the function; it should be relevant, denoting the work or action the function executes. Enclosed in parenthesis, the parameter list specifies the inputs the function will run across. Data is passed into the function by means of parameters, therefore facilitating its operations on that data. The real code carried out upon function calling is within the body of the function. Based on the given parameters, this code specifies the chore the function does.

The capacity of functions in C++ to accept arguments is among their most crucial features since it enables them to run on several sets of data every time they are called. One can pass these arguments—that is, parameters—by value, by reference, or by pointer. Passing by value indicates that the function gets a duplicate of the argument, so any changes made to the parameter inside the function have no effect on the original argument. Conversely, passing by reference indicates that the function runs straight on the original argument and that modifications performed within the function will influence the parameter outside of the function. At last, passing by a pointer gives more control over the data transferred to a variable by allowing a function to access and change its memory address.

In C++, functions can also have return values—that is, they can forward a result back to the calling code upon the completion of their work. Depending on its stated return type, a function may produce several kinds of values. Should a function provide no value, its return type is defined as void. Functions that return values let programmers design more intricate and dynamic applications where the outcome of one action can be passed along to another for additional use.

In C++, functions can be arranged according to their definition and calling behaviour. One often-used distinction is between user-defined and built-in functions. Part of the C++ Standard Library, built-in functions include cin, cout, sqrt, and strlen. These abilities are easily accessible for use without the programmer's definition required. On the other hand, the programmer develops user-defined functions to carry out particular tasks connected to the requirements of the program. One of the main advantages of C++ is its capacity to write custom functions, which lets creators create more adaptive, flexible, and strong applications.

As their name suggests, user-defined functions are ones a programmer defines to satisfy the particular requirements of the project. These tools help programmers to divide difficult chores into smaller, more doable chunks. This division of work facilitates simpler maintenance and debugging as well as readability. When the same chore has to be repeated over several sites within the software, user-defined functions also come in really handy. Defining a function once guarantees that it may be used as many times as required, therefore maintaining the efficiency of the code and lowering the possibility of error introduction.

In C++ programming, a fundamental idea is the ability to classify functions depending on the scope and lifespan of its variables. Local variables are those defined inside a function and available just to that function. They arise from the call to function and vanish after the function ends. Essential for the running of operations, local variables are utilized for temporary data storage. Conversely, global variables—defined outside of any function—are reachable by all other functions in the program. Although global variables might be helpful in some situations, they can also make code more difficult to maintain and debug since they can be changed by any function, thereby making it challenging to follow their values.

Function overloading and function overriding are two other significant differences. Function overloading is the capacity to declare several functions under the same name using different parameter lists. This lets a programmer use the same function name to accomplish comparable chores on many kinds of data. While the functionality differs depending on the arguments given, function overloading improves code clarity and usability since the function name stays constant. Conversely, in C++ object-oriented programming (OOP), function overriding is a capability of derived classes enabling their own implementation of a function previously declared in a base class. In polymorphic behaviour— where objects of various types can call the same function— this is especially helpful as the precise behaviour may vary depending on the object type.

Furthermore, very significant benefits come from the application of functions. Initially, functions serve to lower code duplication. Instead of writing the same code several times, a programmer can use a function defined to do a specific chore anywhere needed. This not only lessens duplication but also helps the program to be more maintainable since updates to the functionality can be done once instead of all through the program. Second, functions increase the code's modularity. Organizing the software into tasks assigned to each responsible party helps one to grasp and change it. Debugging modular codes is also simpler since individual functions may be tested and verified apart from the rest of the program.

Third, functions support the general program readability. Clear, meaningful names for functions help other programmers— who could be reading or maintaining the code going forward— to comprehend the program. Well-named functions act as documentation, therefore lowering the need for long comments and simplifying the code. In big-scale projects, when several people are engaged, and cooperation depends on clear code, this is especially crucial. Functions also facilitate simpler error tracking and debugging. Should a problem develop, it is easier to pinpoint the source by looking at certain operations than by reviewing the whole program.

C++ offers further sophisticated tools connected to functions that increase their adaptability. One such ability is the capacity to pass arguments to other functions. This helps to create higher-order functions that can take other functions as parameters, hence allowing more freedom in program design. When sorting or searching, where the behaviour of a function can be tailored depending on the function provided to it, this function is especially helpful. Function pointers are another advanced tool. In situations where the software must dynamically choose a function at runtime, this can especially be helpful.

Furthermore, supported by C++ is recursion, in which a function may call itself to address smaller, related subproblems, breaking down otherwise difficult problems. Algorithms including divide-and-conquer methods— such as sorting and searching algorithms like Quicksort and merge sort— often use recursion. Although recursion is a useful tool, its ultimate reach to a base case and termination depends on careful design. Recursion used improperly can cause stack overflow problems, in which case too many function calls cause the application to run out of memory.

In C++, the capacity of functions to control complexity, offer flexibility, and enable code reusing defines their power. As a programmer gains competence, the application of functions goes beyond basic chores to solve increasingly complex issues. Programs' performance and functionality can be much improved by the deft application of functions in concert with other C++ tools such as object-oriented programming, templates, and the Standard Template Library (STL).

Finally, a pillar of C++ programming, functions let developers arrange code, cut redundancy, and enhance maintainability by means of organization. Functions make code more modular, simpler to test, and more understandable when a program is broken out into smaller, doable bits. Versatile and supporting sophisticated capabilities such as function overloading, function pointers, and recursion are C++ functions. Any programmer must have a solid grasp of functions since they are a necessary instrument for addressing challenging tasks, enhancing code efficiency, and creating scalable software systems. The value of functions becomes increasingly evident as one keeps learning and developing in C++ since they are fundamental in the design of strong and effective programs.

Scope and Lifetime of Variables

C++ programming calls for a basic knowledge of the ideas of scope and lifetime associated with variables. One must have a strong grasp of these concepts if one is to create free of mistakes, efficient, effective code. Variables come in two flavours: scope and lifespan. While lifetime tells how long a variable will be present while the program is running, scope controls where a variable may be accessed or changed within the program. These two characteristics of variables are inextricably linked to the way memory is allocated, controlled, and deallocated throughout program execution. Understanding the ideas of scope and lifetime helps programmers to create code that is more understandable and maintainable, as well as to properly allocate resources during the program's running. Knowing the relationship between scope and lifetime thoroughly helps a programmer working with C++ construct systems that are error-free and performance-oriented far more easily. This section will examine the scope and lifetime of variables in C++, therefore offering an explanation of the several kinds of scope, the elements influencing the lifetime of variables, and how these ideas are relevant to programming activities carried out in the real world.

Data needed for computation, decision-making, program flow control, and completion of tasks is kept in variables. Any programming language lets you use variables. There are several ways in which C++ defines variables; the placement and method of definition define the scope and lifetime of these variables. Using these ideas will help to ensure that memory is managed properly and that variables are available in the right places. In reference to a variable, the term "scope" describes the area of the program the programming language may view and access for the variable. It directly affects the structure that might be applied to the program and helps to identify the regions in which a variable could be used. Conversely, the term "lifetime" characterizes the length of time a variable stay in memory during the program's running. The lifespan of a variable controls when the variable is formed, when it is destroyed, and for how long it is accessible; hence, it has great relevance.

Variables in the programming language C++ can be arranged by scope and lifespan. These categories closely relate to the position and declaration method of the variables in the program as well as their nature. The most often occurring forms of scopes in the C++ programming language are local, functional, file, and global ones. Every one of these scopes has different guidelines controlling the places where a variable might be accessed and the length of time it stays in memory. Declared inside functions or blocks of code, variables are said to have a local scope. These variables are only accessible within the framework of the function or block in which they are declared. They are created every time the function is called or every time the block runs; they are removed every time the function or block ends. Particularly to variables defined inside a function, the phrase "function scope" is intimately tied to the idea of "local scope." Variables with functional scope are only viewed within the function itself; once the function is completed, they are no longer evident.

Defined outside of all functions, usually at the start of a file, variables defined outside of all functions are not included in the global scope. The fact that these variables are accessible all across the program shows that any function or block of code can benefit from them. Global variables exist throughout the life of the program; they are not deleted until it is closed. Still, too high use of global variables might make debugging and maintaining code challenging. This is so because global variables can be read and changed from anywhere inside the program, so perhaps unintended side effects could follow. Conversely, file scope describes variables declared at the file level but typically limited to the file in which they are stated. This relates to declared at the file level variables. All the functions housed inside the same file can see these variables, but they are invisible to functions housed outside of the file.

Furthermore, the position and way in which variables are defined help one classifies their lifetime in C++. Local variables, which are created inside blocks or functions, have a quite short lifetime. The function or block is allocated when it is first launched; it is released from its allocation when it is ended. This suggests that local variable values are only present for the life of the function or block execution they are connected with, not maintained over numerous function calls or block executions. Local variables help to save memory because of their fleeting character. This is so because once these variables are not needed, the memory used by them releases themselves.

Global variables have a far longer lifespan than this when compared. These parameters are set at the start of the program and remain in memory for the whole running duration of the program. Every operation can access and change global variables; most of the time, these variables are erased upon program termination. Although they should be used rarely since they can pose issues including accidental mutation, namespace pollution, and trouble with debugging and testing, global variables are helpful in some circumstances when data needs to be shared between several departments. One should utilize global variables only seldom. Using function arguments, return values, or class members helps one more effectively distribute data among the several components of object-oriented software.

Furthermore, discussed is a new kind of variable known as stationary variables. Static variables at this point are those that maintain their value even following function calls. Though they are still local to the function in which they are defined, their short-lived existence is not like that of traditional local variables. This is so since they live close to the function always. Static variables are only set once, and their values stay the same for the whole lifetime of the program. Static variables might be useful in situations if you wish to retain information across function calls but do not wish to make the variable global. Although they are most effective for tracking state information specific to a function but should not be lost between invocations, static variables are also helpful for counting function calls or tracking state information.

Furthermore, in C++, operators like new and delete can be used dynamically to allocate variables during program running. Most of the time, these variables are retained in the heap memory and remain there unless explicitly deallocated is done by the delete operator. Unlike local and global variables, which have either automatic or stationary lifetime, dynamically allocated variables have an explicit lifetime under control by the programmer. The programmer must set the memory for these variables during runtime and subsequently guarantee that they are suitably deallocated once they are no longer needed in order to prevent memory leaks. Dynamic memory allocation provides complexity since the programmer must manage the memory explicitly, even if it gives flexibility.

Regarding access control in object-oriented programming (OOP), the idea of variable scope is also absolutely important to address. In the C++ programming language, classes can include member variables ranging from public, private, or protected ones. Public member variables, unlike private and protected member variables, which are limited in terms of accessibility, are available to any code not belonging to the class. Whereas private variables are only available within the class itself, protected variables are allowed to be accessed by both the class itself and any classes inherited from it. The scope of defined member variables in a class is derived from the access modifiers used to define those variables. Strong, safe, and well-structured object-oriented systems depend on a strong awareness of the range of variables included inside classes.

Making suitable use of the scope and lifetime of variables is vitally essential for developing effective C++ programs. Regarding memory use, local variables— variables with a limited scope and a short lifetime— usually prove to be more efficient. This is so because they are created and erased just as needed. Conversely, dynamically allocated and global variables have the possibility to have extended lifetimes, which can lead to a rise in memory usage. Global variables should, however, be used with care since they have the possibility to cause a close linkage between several software components, which in turn makes maintaining and debugging the code more complex. In a perfect world, data should be moved between one function using return values and parameters. This guarantees that only those functions requiring them define the range of variables. As so, the code is easier to understand and reduces the possibility of any negative consequences.

One further important aspect of changeable scope and lifetime that should not be undervalued is memory management. Effective memory consumption in the C++ programming language depends on exact control of the scope and lifespan of variables. For example, memory leaks result from memory allocation but inadequate deallocation. Dynamic memory allocation should be closely watched if too much memory, which would lower performance and, in the worst of cases, cause crashes. Memory should be deallocated as soon as it is not absolutely essential and allocated only when absolutely necessary. The programmer has to make sure that this occurs regularly as well. This helps the application to keep running in an efficient and constant manner.

Local variables— which are automatically allocated and deallocated whenever a function is called and ends— are under management by the system. These variables are stored on the stack, whose limited capacity calls for this. Data that is only temporary in nature is stored in a part of memory, sometimes referred to as the stack. These cover local variables, function parameters, and return addresses. When a function is called, local variables are pushed into the stack; they are removed from the stack upon function termination. This is so since the stack runs always under the last-in, first-out (LIFO) concept. This automatic memory management has one drawback in that it limits the number of variables a function might generate. Still, it increases local variable efficiency. In cases of functions with several local variables or arrays, the stack could overflow and cause issues.

On the flip side, the heap stores dynamically allocated memory. Though it is bigger and more flexible, the heap is a memory area that requires hand administration. When a function ends, memory placed on the heap stays in place unless the programmer specifically releases it by running the delete operator; it is not automatically deallocated. Management of dynamic memory in a suitable configuration is crucial for the prevention of memory leaks and guarantees of program operation. This also comprises deallocating memory when it has been decided it is no longer needed and making sure references to deleted memory are not used, which can produce behaviour not explained.

While the program is running, the lifetime of a variable determines where it may be retrieved at the same time, as it shows how long it will be in existence. Created and destroyed inside functions, local variables provide a simple and efficient approach to controlling memory. Conversely, dynamically allocated memory and global variables allow flexibility but at the cost of possible complexity and memory management challenges. Effective management of variable scope and lifetime helps to assure that memory is used in an efficient manner, lowers the possibility of errors like memory leaks, and helps to produce code that is clean and well-ordered. Understanding these ideas enables programmers to create simpler, understand, debug, and maintain programs, hence producing applications that are more consistent and effective.

Recursion and Practical Implementations

Recursion is a potent and elegant concept used in programming to let a function call itself to solve a problem. One able to call itself is the function of recursion. Many programming languages, notably C++, make substantial application of this idea. Recursion is essentially a method of problem-solving whereby a function solves some of the problems and then assigns the remaining work to itself. By means of this self-referential approach, one may streamline the resolution of challenging problems that would normally call for intricate iterative methods. Recursion is a useful approach in the programming language C++ for handling recurring chores or for handling problems that might be split down into smaller, more like subproblems. Conversely, one needs to have a thorough awareness of how recursion works, its limitations, and the situations in which it could be used if one is to maximize it.

Recursion is predicated on the idea that smaller instances of the same problem can be solved by a function, therefore addressing a problem. The idea rests on this. Every recursive call handle some of the work; in an ideal world, this reduces the problem's size until it reaches a base case— an endpoint where no more recursive calls are needed moving ahead. The recursive calls begin to return as soon as the base case is reached, methodically addressing the problem step-by-step and, lastly, compiling the outcomes to provide the ultimate solution. Two absolutely necessary elements engaged in recursion are the base case and the recursive case. The basis case defines the situation in which the recursion ends. This stops the function from calling itself indefinitely and finally leads to a solution discovered. Dealing with the recursive scenario calls for calling the function once more, but this time with alternative arguments that bring the matter closer to the basic case.

The computation of the factorial of an integer is one instance of recursion deemed to be among the simplest simple. 0! is equivalent to 1; n! is n multiplied by (n-1) multiplied by (n-2) multiplied by... multiplied by 1, and 0! This problem is naturally recursive since the value of n! can be separated down into n * (n-1!). The function will call itself n-1 within the recursive code meant to compute the factorial until it reaches the base case, 0! = 1. Every recursive call made with this self-referential approach reduces the size of the problem, so when the base case is reached, the solution is obtained.

Recursion has certain disadvantages, even if it is conceptually beautiful and usually produces more concise code. The risk of a stack overflow arising from recursion is among its most serious limitations. A bit of the program's call stack is used with every recursive call. Should the recursion be pursued too far, the call stack may overflow, therefore causing the program to malfunction. Recursion is, therefore, most successful when used for problems with a limited recursion depth, which implies that every recursive call works on a smaller portion of the problem. Using an iterative approach could be more successful in circumstances when the depth of recursion is too great. This approach uses a loop to constantly engage in the same tasks without requiring constant calls to the functions. Conversely, for many different types of problems, recursion offers a more natural and direct solution than iterative methods.

Recursion is widely used in the programming language C++ for the aim of fixing problems related to divide-and-conquer algorithms, tree and graph traversals, dynamic programming, and backtracking. Because of their innately recursive structure, the recursive paradigm helps each of these problem areas when more tough issues are reduced to smaller, more doable subproblems. This lets more complex issues be divided into smaller chores. We will look at several instances of useful recursion implementations in C++ in the next sections and discuss how it is applied to address real-world situations.

Among sorting techniques, recursion is clearly one of the most important applications. One such divide-and-conquer method is the quicksort algorithm. This approach partitions an array into smaller subarrays using recursion and then sorts each subarray using another recursion. An element from the array is chosen to be the pivot in Quicksort; subsequently, the array is split so that elements smaller than the pivot are located on the left side and elements greater than the pivot are located on the right side. The technique then recursively arranges the left and right subarrays. This recursive splitting procedure must be kept until every subarray consists of just one element; then, the whole array will be sorted. Elegant and efficient is the sorting method Quicksort uses. Its average time complexity is O(n log n), so its recursive nature helps it to solve problems with enormous data sets.

Searching algorithms also make use of recursion; most famously, binary search is another major subject where it is rather crucial. Binary search is a useful method that one can apply to find a particular member inside a sorted array. The method works by continually splitting the array in half and then deciding whether the element of interest falls left or right half of the array. Should the target be identified, the algorithm produces the index of that target. Should the goal prove elusive, the method will start its search in the suitable half of the array using a recursive approach. Binary search's efficiency stems from each recursive call halving the search space's size in half, hence producing a logarithmic time complexity of O(log n). Binary search is thereby applied for this reason.

Recursion is also a required element in order to address issues involving tree structures, such as tree traversal techniques. A tree is a hierarchical data structure comprising nodes, each with either zero or more child nodes. Recursion in the C++ programming language allows one to frequently do several types of tree traversal—preorder, inorder, postorder, and so on. These traversal techniques enable the function to do a recursive search of each node's left and right subtrees. The function makes particular visits to the tree's nodes in a given sequence. For example, in a preorder traversal, the function will first process the current node, then recursively investigate the left subtree, and lastly traverse the right subtree. Tree architectures are naturally recursive; each subtree is a smaller tree itself; hence, this recursive approach is natural for them. This is, hence, the natural strategy used in tree construction. Thanks to recursion, which simplifies these algorithms to understand and maintain, one can design tree traversal algorithms with clean and readable code.

Furthermore, widely used in dynamic programming— a method of solving problems by breaking them into more doable subproblems and saving the findings to prevent running computations already carried out— recursion is Dynamic programming's use of recursion lets one solve a range of problems, including the computation of Fibonacci numbers, the knapsack problem, and the longest common subsequence. Dynamic programming starts with the concept of optimum substructure. This idea holds that the solutions to the subproblems that make up the more general problem will allow one to deduce the solution to the problem itself. Memorizing—that is, saving the results of subproblems— helps to improve the solution's efficiency by preventing pointless computation. The process of dissecting these challenges into smaller subproblems depends much on recursion.

Another approach to addressing problems is backtracking, which makes very regular use of recursion. Backtracking is applied in the process of resolving problems in which a solution is built in stages. Should a partial solution fail to produce a valid, complete solution, the method will turn back to another and try to solve the problem once more. Backtracking helps one to solve a range of tasks, including the N-Queens problem, solve Sudoku puzzles, and determine all the permutations of a set. These problems use recursion to look at alternative solutions. Should a solution fall short of the criteria, the algorithm will back off and try to fix the issue by means of another path. Because of their recursive character, which makes them efficient in seeking large solution areas, backtracking algorithms are often developed using a depth-first search technique. Another often used tool is backtracking techniques.

Although recursion can help some algorithms be built more easily, it is important to be aware of the situations in which it could not be the most appropriate choice. Especially when the recursion depth is large, deep recursion can cause stack overflow problems. This was discussed earlier in the course. Given that an iterative method does not depend on the call stack and is less likely to produce stack overflow problems, it could be more suited to certain conditions. Furthermore, in terms of the required time or space, recursion might not always provide the most efficient answer. One could find a decent example of this in naive recursive algorithms devoid of memorizing. These techniques might be useless for large inputs since their exponential time complexity suggests. Depending on the situation, either optimizing the recursive approach or transforming it into an iterative process could help to increase its efficiency.

There are several ways in which the programming language C++ offers to maximize recursive algorithms and avoid possible risks. Tail recursion is a method falling into this category whereby the final operation in the function is the recursive call. Tail-recursive operations can be optimized by the compiler such that extra stack frames are not needed. We have achieved this by turning the recursion into an iterative loop. This method is known as tail call optimization or TCO. Though not supported by all compilers, tail call optimization is a helpful tool to be used to improve the efficacy of recursive functions wherever feasible.

Another approach to maximize recursion in C++ is memorization. This approach stores the outputs of recursive calls to stop performing pointless computations. In dynamic programming, which entails solving a lot of subproblems numerous times, memorizing material is quite useful. The outcomes of these subproblems can be stored in an array or hash table when more recursive calls are made. This lets the next calls just search for the saved results instead of having to redo them. This can greatly reduce the time required for the procedure to finish, especially in cases when there are several subproblems.

To sum up, in C++ programming, recursion is a strong and flexible tool. It helps creators to address challenging problems in a neat and simple manner. Among the other fields that would profit from its uses are sorting, searching, tree traversal, dynamic programming, and backtracking. Recursion can provide clean and easy-to-read code, but it's important to have a strong awareness of its constraints— more especially, the danger of stack overflow and, under some conditions, poor performance.

CHAPTER V

Arrays, Pointers, and Dynamic Memory Management

Working with Arrays

Within programming, arrays are a fundamental idea that enables effective data management and storage of collections. Arrays provide a method for methodically organizing and handling several values of the same kind under a single identifier, therefore enabling programmers. Because they offer a straightforward, direct approach to handling memory and analysing vast amounts of data— a chore typical in many programming problems— arrays are especially important in C++. Examining the idea of arrays in C++, this section covers its conception, definition, advantages, constraints, and typical application areas. It also looks at sophisticated array operations and techniques as well as methods for best using arrays in practical applications.

In C++, arrays are continuous blocks of memory holding a set number of the same type of components. Once declared, an array's items are kept in sequential memory regions, which provides quick access depending on their index. Starting at 0 for the first element and rising by one for every next element, the index— also known as the subscript— gives For an array designed to hold five integers, for example, the first element can be accessed with index 0, the second element with index 1, and so on, up to index 4. With an index serving as a guide to every element, the array in this example would have the form array[0], array[1], array[2], array[3], and array[4].

Because they let programmers operate on several values with minimum overhead, arrays are a fundamental data structure in C++. An array offers a neat and efficient method to cluster related data rather than establishing several independent variables. When working with a lot of data, like in numerical calculations or processing input and output in applications involving significant data handling, arrays are especially helpful. By permitting direct modification of adjacent memory blocks, arrays offer a way to maximize memory use. One of the main benefits of arrays— especially for applications with speed sensitivity— is their effectiveness in memory management.

Declaring an array in C++ requires careful definition of its size, as once the array is produced, its size is fixed. For instance, an array meant to hold 10 integers has to be declared with its size clear. C++ arrays are statically allocated; hence the number of members in the array cannot be altered during runtime, unlike higher-level languages supporting dynamic arrays. This restriction forces developers to give much thought to the array's compile time size. C++ does, however, also offer a more flexible means of working with dynamic arrays utilizing pointers, which enables memory allocation during runtime. In C++, dynamic arrays can be produced with the new keyword and resized as necessary by memory reallocation. Though it adds more complexity to memory management, this method provides more flexibility than static arrays.

Working with arrays in C++ also depends critically on the initializing process for arrays. Depending on the particular requirements of the program, C++ allows one to start arrays in many ways. Starting an array with specified values for its elements is the most often used approach at declaration. An array of integers, for instance, may be started with certain values like so: int arr[] = {1, 2, 3, 4, 5};. Alternatively, curly braces with empty values allow arrays to be set to default values— such as zeros— by int arr[5] = {};, therefore rendering all entries of the array zero. Should the size of the array be explicitly stated during initialization— as in int arr[5] = {1, 2, 3, 4, 5};, the array will have the designated values and any remaining items will be zero. Apart from that, arrays can be started one element at a time by means of loops or by explicitly assigning values to particular indices following array declaration.

Arrays in C++ have significant restrictions, even if they are really helpful. Static arrays have one of the disadvantages: their fixed size. The array cannot be resized without reallocation or redefining after it is declared with a specific size. This can cause problems in initiatives involving dynamic user input or reading from vast data files if the precise amount of data is unknown in advance. In some situations, dynamic arrays or other data structures— such as vectors (part of the Standard Template Library or STL in C++)— may be more appropriate since they enable resizing during runtime. Vectors automatically control array size, therefore giving the programmer the freedom to add or delete elements as necessary. Though their dynamic character causes additional memory overhead compared to arrays, vectors are a popular choice for many

C++ developers because they provide dynamic scaling and simplicity of use.

Memory management is yet another crucial factor while working with arrays. Accessing array elements is usually faster than accessing elements in other data structures using more complicated memory allocation schemes since arrays are contiguous blocks of memory. But sometimes, especially if the array isn't completely used, the continuous character of arrays causes wasted memory. For instance, the remaining 90 elements in an array are defined with 100 components, but only 10 elements are occupied wastefully by memory. One of the reasons dynamic arrays and data structures like linked lists are usually used in situations where the volume of data is quite variable is this inefficacy. On the other hand, arrays are ideal for circumstances whereby the size of the data collection is known in advance and stays constant.

Accessing elements in an array is simple since elements are kept consecutively in consecutive memory addresses. One of the main benefits of arrays is this effective random access to any element. Arranging an array of numbers, arr[0], arr[1], and so on, allows one to access each element by indicated index in square braces. For many uses, including numerical computations, matrix operations, and sorting algorithms, the capacity to access elements in constant time, O(1) makes arrays quite efficient. Furthermore, arrays let one iterate through their elements using loops— a typical practice accomplished with either a for loop or a while loop. Whether it is for searching, organizing, or data transformation, iteration lets developers work on every component in an array.

Working with arrays in C++ requires making sure the application does not try to access elements outside the array's bounds since this could result in crashes or uncertain behaviour. C++ does not automatically check boundaries for array accesses; thus, the programmer must be careful not to read invalid indices. Accessing an array element with an index outside the valid range— that is, less than zero or larger than or equal to the size of the array— will cause memory to be accessed that does not belong to the array, therefore producing erratic behaviour. This is a main disadvantage of arrays in C++ since the absence of bounds checking forces the programmer to be alert in guaranteeing that the indices used for array access are legitimate.

From storing and organizing massive databases to running intricate algorithms, arrays in C++ have numerous useful uses. Arrays find frequent application in sorting systems. Simple implementation of several sorting methods— including bubble sort, quicksort, and merge sort— is made possible using arrays. Usually involving comparison and exchanging elements within an array until the components are in the intended sequence, sorting techniques Because their elements are readily available and may be effectively changed, arrays' simplicity makes them perfect for running these techniques. Furthermore, often employed in searching systems, including binary and linear searches, to locate particular elements or values inside a dataset, are arrays. Fast access to elements depending on their index made possible by arrays is essential for the effectiveness of search activities.

Matrix operations— that is, mathematical calculations or image processing— also find use for arrays. Many times, matrices are portrayed as two-dimensional arrays where every element relates to a value in the matrix. Nestled loops let one effectively run operations, including matrix multiplication, addition, and transposition across the rows and columns of the array. Large volumes of data must be handled and controlled in a methodical manner in computational activities, including simulations, scientific computing, and data analysis; hence, arrays can also be employed in these fields.

Finally, one of the most crucial and flexible data structures in C++, arrays offer a strong way to arrange and control groups of data. Their limited size, quick access, and effective memory allocation make them appropriate for many uses, particularly in situations when the volume of data is known in advance and stays constant. Arrays do, however, also have several drawbacks, namely their constant size and absence of bounds checking, which, if improperly managed, could cause inefficiencies and mistakes. Dynamic arrays and other data structures— such as vectors— that give more flexibility in managing variable-sized datasets allow C++ to get above these restrictions. Since arrays are fundamental to many methods and applications, C++ programmers must be able to know when and how to use them. Whether for sorting, searching or sophisticated data manipulation, arrays remain a fundamental tool in the C++ programmer's toolkit, therefore enabling effective and efficient data management.

Introduction to Pointers

One of the most useful tools in the C++ programming language, pointers give writers direct access to memory and let them finely control and alter data. Mastery of C++ depends on an awareness of pointers since many advanced programming approaches are based on them. The idea of pointers in C++ is investigated in this section together with its definition, working mechanisms, and reasons for use in different programming contexts. It also looks at pointer-related operations— memory management, pointer arithmetic, and the link between pointers and arrays. By means of this investigation, readers will get a thorough grasp of pointers and their efficient application in C++.

Fundamentally, a pointer is a variable whose memory address is another variable. A pointer maintains the address in memory where a value is found rather than a direct value, such as an integer or a floating-point number. This basic idea lets programmers dynamically allocate memory during runtime, pass huge structures to functions effectively, and indirectly access and change variables. Like an address on a map, a pointer points to the position of an object in memory rather than a real thing.

Pointers declared in C++ are indicated by the kind of variable they will point to, then by an asterisk (*). Declaring a pointer to an integer, for instance, would have the syntax int* ptr;. The asterisk notes that the variable is a pointer to an integer rather than an integer itself. Once a pointer is declared, the address-of operator (&) allows one to assign it the address of a variable. For an integer variable x, for example, we may allocate its address to the pointer ptr with the statement ptr = &x; Here, &x is the variable x's memory location housed in the pointer.

C++'s pointers have various benefits. The capacity to directly control memory is one of the main advantages. Pointers let software access and change variables housed in separate memory regions. When working with big datasets or complicated data structures, including arrays, linked lists, and trees— which allow for effective memory use and manipulation— this is very helpful. Pointers also allow dynamic memory allocation, which is absolutely essential when compile time's unknown data volume calls for. By means of the new and delete operators, C++ enables dynamic allocation and deallocation of memory during runtime, therefore offering great degrees of control over memory management.

Pointers also have another important benefit in that they can provide variables to functions by reference instead of by value. Usually given by value in C++, function arguments produce a copy of the parameter upon function call. For big data structures, such as arrays or objects, this can be ineffective since replicating the whole structure can take time and use memory extensively. Passing parameters using pointers allows a function to access the original data straight-forwardly, therefore saving the need to produce a copy of the variable. When the function must alter the original data, this is very helpful since changes made to the data inside the function also show outside of the function.

Though they have significant benefits, pointers in C++ are rather complicated. Managing memory correctly and avoiding memory-related mistakes, including memory leaks and segmentation faults, presents the most important obstacle with pointers. C++ lets programmers personally control memory; hence, it is their job to make sure memory is allocated and deallocated correctly. Ignoring this could cause dangling pointers— where a pointer points to memory that has previously been deallocated— or memory leaks, in which memory is allocated but never destroyed. In C++ programs, these shortcomings could cause erratic behaviour, crashes, and performance concerns.

Knowing the several pointer-related operations in C++ helps one to avoid such problems. Dereferencing— accessing the value kept at the memory address the pointer points to— is among the most fundamental activities in computers. One accomplishes this with the dereference operator (*). If ptr is a pointer to an integer, for instance, *ptr is the value kept at the memory location pointed at by ptr. Dereferencing lets a software change the value kept at that memory location. If ptr points to a variable x, for example, we can dereference the pointer and assign a fresh value: *ptr = 10;.

Another crucial idea in C++ that lets one modify pointers depending on their position in memory is pointer arithmetic. Pointers can be raised or lowered to traverse memory sites since they save memory addresses. A pointer increment goes to the next memory address matching the type of data the pointer is pointing to. For instance, a pointer pointing to an integer will point to the next integer in memory— usually four bytes away— should it be incrementally changed. Arrays and other data structures can be traversed using pointer arithmetic, but it should be done carefully to prevent accessing memory outside of boundaries, which would cause unknown behaviour.

In dynamic memory allocation in C++, pointers are also quite important. Dynamic memory allocation at runtime, made possible by the new operator, lets a program create variables or arrays whose size is decided during execution rather than compile time. The returning pointer to the allocated memory by the new operator allows one to access and work on the allocated data. Dynamic allocation of an array of integers, for instance, would be accomplished with the statement int* arr = new int[size], where size is the array's total count. The delete operator has to deallocate the memory once it is no longer required to stop memory leaks. For instance, deallocates the memory allocated to the array arr.

In C++ programming, the idea of a memory leak— that is, dynamically allocated memory not adequately deallocated— is a frequent problem. Program use of too much memory resulting from memory leaks could degrade performance and finally cause system failure. Dynamic memory allocation and deallocation must be tightly managed if one is to stop memory leaks. Smart pointers— part of the Standard Library— are generally advised in current C++ to automatically control memory and stop leaks. By guaranteeing that memory is deallocated when it is no longer needed, smart pointers— such as std::unique_ptr and std::shared_ptr— manage memory automatically, therefore lowering the possibility of memory leaks.

Another crucial element of handling pointers in C++ is the idea of "null pointers." A null pointer is a pointer devoid of any accessible legitimate memory location. It is frequently used to show that a pointer is purposefully set to an erroneous value or that it has not yet been initialized. Safer and more explicit than using NULL or 0 as a null pointer, a null pointer is expressed in C++ using the constant nullptr. In situations when a pointer is intended to be assigned a legitimate memory address later in the program but at that moment it does not yet point to a valid place, null pointers are frequently employed. Before they are dereferenced, null pointers should be checked, as dereferencing them causes unpredictable behaviour and usually causes segmentation faults.

When working with arrays in C++, pointers are also somewhat extensively utilized. Actually, since the name of an array in C++ is effectively a pointer to the first member of the array, arrays in C++ are tightly related to pointers. Effective array manipulation made possible by this link between arrays and pointers via pointer arithmetic is Incrementing a pointer pointing to an array element, for instance, will let you access the element that follows in the array. Furthermore, arrays can be supplied to functions as pointers, therefore enabling the function to directly alter the components of the original array instead of dealing with a copy of the array.

In object-oriented programming (OOP), dynamic memory for objects is often managed, and polymorphism is implemented via pointers to objects. Classes and objects can be generated dynamically with pointers in C++; these pointers are then frequently used to call methods or access member variables of the objects they point to. Using the new operator, dynamic memory allocation for objects is accomplished; objects may be deallocated with the delete operator. Working with pointers to objects calls for careful management of the memory to avoid dangling pointers and memory leaks, though.

Moreover, the use of some data structures, including linked lists, trees, and graphs, depends on pointers absolutely. These data structures enable effective data traversal and manipulation by means of pointers connecting individual elements, therefore enabling. Whereas each node in a linked list has a pointer to the next node in the list, in trees, each node may have pointers to several child nodes. Many methods and applications depend on dynamic, flexible storage and retrieval of data, which these data structures enable by means of pointers.

Finally, pointers are a great and flexible tool of C++ that gives developers direct access to memory, therefore enabling effective data manipulation and application of advanced programming approaches. Programmers can fully leverage C++ for effective, low-level programming by knowing how pointers operate, how to perform pointer arithmetic, how to manage dynamic memory, and how to prevent frequent hazards, including memory leaks and dangling pointers. Essential for learning C++ and developing high-performance programs, pointers form the foundation of the language. Pointers are still an essential tool for developers despite their complexity; they help them to produce more flexible, strong, and efficient applications. By using precise and deliberate pointer use, C++ programmers can maximize their applications for memory management and performance as well as increase program control.

Dynamic Memory Allocation

Since it helps programmers to effectively manage memory while the program is executing, dynamic memory allocation is a basic need in C++ programming.

Greater flexibility is provided by dynamic memory allocation than by static memory allocation, which is typified by a fixed amount of memory upon compilation. Dynamic memory allocation lets memory be allocated and deallocated running-through. This ability is essential for the development of efficient algorithms able to control various data volumes without knowing the total quantity of the data ahead of time. Dynamic memory allocation is a great technique to avoid errors, including memory leaks, segmentation faults, and undefined behaviour; nonetheless, it needs careful control to maximize its usefulness. In C++, it is usual practice to split memory into two separate categories: heap and stack memory. Stack memory is used for the static memory allocation in cases when the size of data structures is known at the time of compilation. In terms of dynamic memory allocation, heap memory is used somewhat differently. Runtime brings this kind of memory allocation. Stack memory is maintained automatically by the compiler; heap memory must be explicitly handled by the programmer. Stack memory is controlled automatically by the compiler; hence, this difference is important. Dynamic memory allocation is controlled by the new and delete operators in C++, which lets the programmer request and release heap memory. Dynamic memory allocation helps one to accomplish this.

The new operator needs to be used initially to allocate memory on the heap, therefore starting the process of dynamic memory allocation. The new operator requests a specific size of the memory block and then returns a pointer pointing at the beginning of the allocated memory block. For a single object, for instance, the syntax for allocating memory is this: pointer = new type;, in which case type is the object allocated's data type. The memory that is specifically deallocated by the delete operator is set aside until the memory allocated by the new one is purposefully deactivated. This method enables one to use memory in a more flexible and efficient way; hence, it is especially helpful in cases when the size of data structures is unknown at the time of compilation or varies while the program is running.

Among the most important benefits of dynamic memory allocation is its capacity to let programs change in response to changing memory needs while they are being used. Dynamic memory allocation allows you, for example, to store a variable number of elements in a data structure. This lets the program set just enough memory for the needed data. Both of which involve circumstances in which the total quantity of the data is unknown at the time of compilation, the administration of user input, and working with large datasets are scenarios in which this is particularly beneficial. If dynamic memory allocation were not possible, developers would have to allocate memory in a fixed way. This could result in either too little or too much memory for the needed data or an overuse of memory overall.

Conversely, dynamic memory allocation results in another degree of complexity that must be under control, especially with reference to ensuring memory is deallocated in a suitable way, which is one of the most important challenges when it is no longer needed. Memory allocated by the new operator must be explicitly relinquished using the delete operator if one wants to stop memory leaks in C++. Maintaining track of all the dynamically allocated memory and ensuring it is deallocated when it is not in use is absolutely vital for programmers. Prevention of memory leaks depends on this habit.

Debugging memory leaks can be especially difficult since they often do not produce instantly occurring issues. Rather, as the program keeps using memory without releasing it, it causes a steady drop in performance over time. C++ offers smart pointers— a feature of the Standard

Template Library (STL)— as a way to help prevent memory leaks. Smart pointers are a type of pointer that, when memory is no longer needed, automatically manages it by guaranteeing deallocation. This guarantees no wasted RAM. Two versions of smart pointers primarily used in C++ are std::unique_ptr and std::shared_ptr. Automatic dynamic memory management is accomplished using these smart pointers. By means of smart pointers, developers may reduce the possibility of memory leaks and ensure that memory is under competent and safe management.

Another important element of dynamic memory allocation is the idea of "dancing pointers". A "dangling pointer" is the state whereby a pointer keeps addressing a memory location that has been deallocated or is no longer the legitimate location. Dereferencing a dangling reference can produce any one of undetermined behaviour, crashes, or data damage. Once the memory that pointers point to has been deallocated, it is imperative to make sure they are set to nullptr to avoid dangling pointers from resulting. This method guarantees that any attempt to dereference the pointer will produce a safe and predictable outcome, such as a null pointer exception, therefore ensuring the success of any such endeavour.

Apart from its use for the allocation of memory for individual objects, dynamic memory allocation allows memory to be assigned for arrays. The new operator can allocate a sufficiently substantial portion of memory to allow for an array of objects. One can use the syntax pointer = new type[size] to create memory for an array of size elements of type, for example. This is particularly useful in cases when, at compilation, the exact count of the elements in the array is unknown. Nonetheless, dynamically created arrays must be deallocated by the delete operator whenever they are no longer needed if we are to guarantee efficient memory management.

Dynamic memory allocation is also rather crucial for the application of data structures such as linked lists, trees, and graphs. These data structures must be able to dynamically allocate memory for individual elements if they are to allow the data to expand or contract. For instance, the new operator is usually used dynamically to allocate every node in a linked list. Given the node has a pointer to the subsequent node in the list, the program can move and change the list in line with its needs. These data structures give a great degree of efficiency and flexibility since they allow components to be added or removed depending on the use of dynamic memory allocation, therefore enabling growth and decrease in size.

Dynamic memory allocation is quite essential if we are to effectively create algorithms requiring the modification of large datasets. For instance, sorting and searching techniques usually operate on large arrays or other data structures requiring dynamic allocation whilst the method is being used. These methods would be limited by the constant size of static arrays in the absence of dynamic memory allocation, so managing datasets of varying sizes would prove difficult. By means of dynamic memory allocation, which also guarantees efficient memory allocation, the program can adapt to the volume of the data.

Furthermore, the C++ programming language has some capabilities meant to help developers better control dynamic memory. One instance of such a feature is found in the STL under its std::vector container. The std::vector dynamic array dynamically changes its size to suit the added or deleted members as elements are added or deleted. Standard vectors manage memory automatically, unlike most arrays. This guarantees that the program's needs guide memory allocation and deallocation. This eliminates the need for developers to manually allocate and deallocate memory for arrays, so it is a safer and more practical substitute for raw pointers. Arrays are thus a safer option.

Apart from the std::vector container, the STL in C++ provides several more containers that can be applied to control dynamic memory. These containers cover std::list, std::deque, and std::map. Higher-level abstraction these containers provide for dynamic memory management helps developers focus on the logic of their applications instead of having to worry about memory allocation and deallocation. Still, there are situations when raw pointer based manual dynamic memory management is needed. This is particularly true whether optimizing for efficiency or working with low-level data structures.

Performance is significantly influenced by memory management; hence while using dynamic memory allocation, one must keep this in mind. Dynamic memory allocation can be slower than stack-based memory allocation since it involves the more difficult process of memory from the heap. This is so since the heap has a more complicated construction. Furthermore, too strong memory allocation and deallocation can lead to fragmentation— a type of memory allocation in which small blocks allocated in a non-contiguous fashion generate inefficiencies. To maximize memory use and so lower the impact that dynamic memory allocation has on performance to the greatest extent possible, one must carefully manage memory, allocate and deallocate memory only when it is absolutely necessary, and take into account using techniques such as memory pools or custom allocators.

Memory fragmentation is a typical issue with dynamic memory that results from working with This issue results from a small chunk distribution of free memory on the heap that does not follow a consecutive pattern. Memory being allocated and deallocated creates gaps of free memory that develop over time. Since they are generated over time, these gaps could not be significant enough to satisfy fresh memory allocation needs. This could lead to slower performance and ineffective memory use. One approach to help minimize fragmentation is memory pools, pre-allocated blocks of memory that can be split up into smaller pieces depending on the need. Using memory pools provides a more efficient way of allocating and deallocating memory, therefore reducing the likelihood of fragmentation.

Dynamic memory allocation is a significant ability of C++ that helps memory management that is both flexible and efficient throughout the running of a program. By use of the new and delete operators, programmers can dynamically allocate and deallocate memory. This helps them to manage different data volumes. Dynamic memory allocation does, however, also produce problems such as memory leaks, dangling pointers, and fragmentation, all of which must be carefully regulated if we are to ensure the stability and performance of the application. By using dynamic memory allocation, programmers in C++ can create quick, high-performance applications competent in handling complicated data structures and algorithms. Smart pointers, memory management strategies, and high-level containers such as std::vector help one to construct these programs. Dynamic memory allocation is a must-have feature for developers since it may greatly increase the flexibility and capability of C++ applications. Dynamic memory allocation can achieve this by closely observing memory management techniques.

CHAPTER VI

Object-Oriented Programming (OOP) in C++

Classes and Objects

Class and object concepts are among C++'s basic building blocks for object-oriented programming (OOP). These ideas let developers of real-world items and behaviours replicate them in a way that makes software development more scalable, maintainable, and understandable. By means of classes and objects, C++ helps to create intricate data structures that capture both data and functionality, therefore enabling developers to produce more ordered and modular code. The basic ideas of classes and objects in C++, their importance in object-oriented design, and their pragmatic use in creating strong software programs will be discussed in this section.

First of all, one must grasp the interactions among classes and objects. A class is a user-defined data type functioning as an object creation blueprint. It specifies the traits (data members) and actions (member functions) the produced objects will exhibit. Consider a class as a blueprint or template for a house: although the blueprint itself is not a house, it outlines the number of rooms, doors, and windows of the house, therefore guiding its construction. In the same vein, a class specifies the behaviour and structure its objects will display, but the class itself does not occupy memory space until it is instantiated as an object.

Conversely, an object is a case study of a class. It is a particular entity with a class-defined data capacity that takes up memory. An object is produced when a class is instantiated and has real data matching the characteristics stated by the class. Objects interact by invoking functions (methods) described in their respective classes; they are real-world entities— cars, workers, books, etc. If your class is called a Car, for instance, every object in that class can depict an individual car with its own distinct characteristics— colour, make, and model— as well as its own behaviours— starting, halting, or accelerating.

Classes in C++ are stated with the class keyword. This keyword indicates to the compiler that a fresh data type is under creation. Usually, a class consists of two primary components: the member functions and the data members. While member functions specify the tasks an object may do, data members are variables that retain the state or properties of an object. In a Car class, for instance, the data members may be colour, make, model, and year; the member functions would be start(), stop(), and accelerate(). These elements, taken together, capture the state and the behaviour of the objects created by the class.

Emphasizing the bundling of data and the techniques operating on that data into a single unit, encapsulation is one of the most crucial characteristics of classes and objects. Encapsulation guarantees control of access to an object and protection of its internal state. A class can conceal its internal implementation details from outside code by making data members private and granting public access or modification capability. This facilitates the maintenance of the class and increases its modular character. A class might let a user alter the colour of a Car object, for instance, but it will not let direct access to the underlying memory storing the colour. Rather, the user interacts with the class by means of its public methods, which govern data access and modification.

Encapsulation also supports the fundamental idea in object-oriented design— that of information hiding. Information concealing guarantees that, while internal or internal details are concealed, only required information about the functioning of an object is revealed to the outside world. This lessens the complexity of interactions among things, hence improving design. When interacting with a Car object, for instance, the user only has to know how to start and stop the engine; he or she does not need knowledge of internal engine operation. This abstraction lets the developer change the internal operations of the class without influencing its outward use, hence simplifying interactions with objects.

Inheritance— which lets a class inherit characteristics and actions from another class— is another fundamental aspect of object-oriented programming. This function lets one build a hierarchy of classes whereby a derived class inherits the traits of a base class but can also have extra ability. Inheritance advances code reuse and helps to lower code duplication. In a program that represents several kinds of automobiles, for example, you might have a base class named Vehicle with shared characteristics such as speed and fuel capacity as well as common actions like start() and stop(). A derived class called Car might inherit from Vehicle, so it would automatically have all of Vehicle's characteristics but could also have its own unique ones, such as air conditioning or number of doors. Reusing the code in Vehicle without having to replicate it, the Car class can inherit from the Vehicle class.

One of the fundamental ideas in inheritance is polymorphism— that is, the capacity of a class to adopt several forms. Virtual functions and function overriding help to accomplish polymorphism in C++. Polymorphism preserves the particular behaviours of objects of distinct kinds while allowing their treatment as objects of a shared base class. This helps a computer to consistently process objects of various kinds, even if their particular behaviour is unique. If your parent class Vehicle has a virtual function move(), for instance, both the Car and Truck derived classes can override the move() function to apply their own particular behaviour for how they move. Notwithstanding these variations, you can treat both Car and Truck objects as instances of Vehicles and use the move() function polymorphically, therefore enabling the proper version of the function to be used depending on the real type of the object.

Apart from inheritance and polymorphism, C++ has multiple inheritance, a capability enabling a class to inherit from several base classes. In some situations, when a class must inherit traits from several sources, this ability can be helpful. Multiple inheritance can, therefore, also bring complications, including possible conflicts between the base classes and uncertainty in method resolution. C++ offers virtual inheritance to help reduce these problems, therefore guaranteeing that the most derived class has a single, unambiguous base class.

Crucially important elements of C++ classes are constructors and destructors. An automatically called special member function called a constructor is what an object instantiation triggers. Its main goal is to start the data members of the object to have legitimate values.

Constructors can be overloaded; therefore, a class can have several constructors with varying parameter lists to enable several approaches to object creation. A Car class might, for instance, include a parameterized constructor that lets the user indicate the car's manufacturer, model, and year of manufacture, as well as a default constructor that starts the car with default values.

Conversely, a destructor is a specific member function triggered upon an object expressly removed or outside of scope. Any resources the object could have acquired during its lifetime— memory or file handles, among other things— are released by the destructor. Managing dynamic memory allocation and guarantees that resources are correctly cleaned up when objects are no longer required to depend on destroyers. While they can be directly activated using the delete operator in the case of dynamically allocated objects, destructors in C++ are automatically called when objects fall out of sight.

Classes in C++ can also enable operator overloading, therefore enabling developers to modify operator behaviour for objects of a class. This ability lets objects of user-defined kinds be handled with the same syntax and operators as built-in types. You might overload the + operator, for instance, therefore letting items of a ComplexNumber class be joined together with the + sign. Because it lets developers utilize known operators in the framework of their own classes, operator overloading helps make code clearer and more intuitive.

The absence of object-oriented programming is another crucial idea. Abstraction is hiding the core implementation and simplifying difficult systems by presenting just the pertinent elements. Classes in C++ let the developer specify the public interface of a class while hiding its internal implementation details, therefore offering a natural method of implementing abstraction. This division of issues facilitates maintainability, understanding, and extension of codes. The Car class might reveal a public method start() for instance, which lets users start the car without knowing the specifics of internal engine operation. The start() method's abstraction away from the user helps to simplify and clarify the class for use.

In essence, object-oriented programming in C++ is based on classes and objects, which are also absolutely vital for creating manageable, scalable, and strong software. C++ lets developers build sophisticated systems that are both modular and easy to expand by grouping data and action within classes. C++ offers strong means for code reuse, flexibility, and maintainability by means of inheritance, polymorphism, and abstraction. Mastery of C++ and the development of efficient object-oriented solutions to practical issues depend on an awareness of classes and objects. Using classes and objects, developers can produce quite dependable and efficient software systems with great attention to design ideas such as encapsulation and abstraction.

Constructors, Destructors, and Inheritance

C++ takes advantage of three fundamental concepts of object-oriented programming. These ideas are inheritance, constructions, and destroyers. These ideas help programmers to produce modular, adaptable, and manageable code. These ideas provide the basis and help to define and control the behaviour and lifetime of objects inside a program. By using these ideas, developers can create classes that can effectively manage resource allocation and deallocation, as well as enable code reuse and extension. Designed to be a complex and reliable programming language, C++ can be used to produce challenging applications. Every one of these traits is essential in enabling C++ to be what it is now. We shall look at the basic ideas underlying constructors, destructors, and inheritance in the C++ programming language in the next paragraphs. We will also investigate the usefulness of these ideas as well as their pragmatic implementations and interactions to provide effective memory and resource management inside object-oriented systems.

Constructors are a kind of special member function used automatically anytime an object is created in the C++ programming language to start things. A constructor's basic goal is to assign appropriate values and start the data members of an object. This helps to ensure that, upon first usage, the object is in a consistent condition. The constructor's name exactly matches the name of the class to which it fits. Not even void objects— constructors have no return value. Constructors are widely used in the programming language C++ for resource allocation including memory, file opening, or variable initializing needs. By use of them, developers can exercise control over the configuration of an object and ensure that it starts its life in a well defined and predictable manner.

Constructors can be overloaded; therefore, a class can have many constructors, each with a unique set of parameters. This feature allows developers to provide a range of several approaches for the building of objects depending on the needs of the program. A class might have, for example, a parameterized constructor— which allows the user to define custom values for the data members of the object at the time of creation— and a default constructor— which is in charge of starting an object with basic values. Constructor overloading is particularly useful in cases when objects can be created in several ways depending on the current conditions.

Regarding dynamic memory allocation, the constructor mechanism included in C++ is also really important. Usually known as dynamically allocated memory, the constructor can utilize the new operator to allocate suitable memory space whenever an object requires it from the heap. This allocation may be quite crucial while working with data structures like linked lists, arrays, or trees where the amount of the data cannot be known before compilation. The constructor of the class permits memory to be allocated, therefore enabling the class to ensure that the necessary resources are available at the moment of the object creation.

Conversely, a destructor in C++ is a particular member function executed automatically whether an object is erased purposefully or when it departs the program's reach. A destructor's basic goal is to release any resources the object could have accrued over its lifetime. Should an object open a file or dynamically allocated memory, the destructor's job is to tidy up those resources prior to object destruction. Thoughtfully built destructors will help to prevent memory leaks and other resource management issues when objects are no longer needed.

Because of their particular function, destructors are extremely important in applications using dynamic memory allocation. If correct destruction is not done, dynamically allocated memory may remain reserved long after the object has been destroyed. Memory leaks, thereby exposing the system to weakness. Thanks to the delete operator— which C++ offers— memory that was previously allocated with the new operator can be released. Usually, the site of this deallocation is the destructor. This guarantees that resources are liberated in a suitable way and that the software does not waste memory.

Destructors are likewise not able to be overloaded using constructors, much as constructors lack a return type. A class can only have one destructor; this is the one called upon automatically each time an item of that class is destroyed. The destructor is automatically triggered in the case that an object is destroyed when its scope of operation is compromised— that is, when it is a local variable included in the function. Should the object be dynamically allocated using the new operator during the creation phase, the destructor is triggered upon object elimination using the delete operator. Correct memory management with destructors is vitally required for creating stable and efficient C++ programs.

Inheritance is another fundamental element of object-oriented programming in C++ since it allows one to generate new classes from an existing collection of classes. It enables one class to inherit traits and behaviours from another class, therefore promoting the reuse of code and, hence, lessening repetition. By means of inheritance, a derived class can acquire the characteristics (data members and member functions) of a base class. This method also lets the derived class alter or expand the behaviours of the parent class. Options open to the derived class are additional data members, new member functions, or the ability to override current base class functionalities.

Inheritance in C++ is among the most crucial instruments available for simulating the interactions among real-world objects. It makes it possible to build class hierarchies. Consider a program that models numerous types of vehicles, for example. A basic class called Vehicle may thus explain common behaviours and traits, including acceleration() and braking() functions, as well as common properties such as speed, fuel type, and colour. A derived class known as a Car might inherit the Vehicle class and then enhance the Vehicle by adding characteristics unique to vehicles, such as the engine type or number of doors. This will enable the Car class to have access to all the traits and behaviours connected with the Vehicle class as well as to offer its own unique features only for cars.

Inheritance is among Object-oriented design's most fundamental ideas. This is so because inheritance allows one to generate more specialized classes without resorting to duplicate code. The ultimate effect is more compact and simpler to maintain code. A derived class gains access to the members of the base class that are both public and protected instantaneously upon inheriting from a base class. Object-oriented programming depends critically on encapsulation since it keeps the object from directly accessing private members of the base class. This is among the factors explaining the great importance of encapsulation. Giving access specifiers that combine public and protected access requirements allows the base class to identify which features of its implementation are passed on to derived classes.

One of the most significant benefits of inheritance is the capacity to supersede the roles of particular members. Function overriding is exemplified when a derived class offers its own implementation of a function previously specified in the base class. In C++, function overriding can be performed by first re-implementing the function within the class derived from the base class after using the virtual keyword within the function of the base class. This makes polymorphic behaviour feasible. This implies that the suitable override method will be called at runtime depending on the actual object type since a pointer or reference to a base class might point to objects of derived classes. Polymorphism makes it feasible to create more flexible and adaptable code by letting new derived classes enter the scene without calling for a code modification interacting with the base class.

The constructor of the derived class is called first, and thereafter, the constructor of the base class is called while a derived class is under construction. This confirms that the base class has been correctly instantiated at the start of the process before the derived class may be started. In case a derived class is needed to offer parameters to the constructor of the source class, one can take advantage of an initializer list. In the same sense, the destructor of a derived class is first, then the destructor of the base class when the derived class is destroyed. This ensures that the resources allocated by the base class are released in a suitable way once the derived class has completed cleaning its own resources.

Inheritance falls into several different types depending on the number of base classes a derived class inherits from. In C++, the idea of many inheritances is used to explain the mechanism by which a derived class could inherit many base classes. Multiple inheritance allows a class to inherit traits from several other classes, which might be helpful in some situations. Multiple inheritance, on the other hand, can also cause problems, including uncertainty, should the base classes have member names or functionalities that contradict each other. Virtual inheritance is a concept provided by the computer language C++ that guarantees the most derived class only inherits one copy of a common base class. This is carried out to stop these issues from developing. Virtual inheritance helps to reduce some of the problems connected with multiple inheritance. Ensuring that derived classes share a single instance of the base class helps one to accomplish this.

Still another aspect of inheritance in the C++ programming language is being able to regulate the visibility of inherited members. A derived class can control whether or not the members it inherits from a base class are available from outside the class when it inherits from the base class. Inherited by default as public and protected members of the derived class, respectively, are members of the base class who are public and those who are protected. Conversely, access specifiers enable the derived class to change its behaviour should the chance present itself. A derived class, for example, can show that a member function inherited from a base class should be kept private or protected, therefore restricting access to the method from outside the class structure.

In essence, object-oriented programming in the C++ programming language requires constructors, destructors, and inheritance— fundamental components. Constructors ensure that objects start in a valid state and enable the proper initialization of objects, therefore ensuring their validity. The deallocation of resources— which also helps to prevent memory leaks and resource waste— is under the purview of destroyers. Inheritance helps derived classes to inherit from base classes therefore permitting the creation of class hierarchies resembling the relationships found in the real world. This thus motivates the structural reusing of code and its application. Strong features provided by the programming language C++ help one to create flexible and extendable programs. These techniques comprise function overriding, inheritance, and polymorphism. When used properly, these features enable one to develop well-structured, easily maintained programs and to properly manage resources. Learning object-oriented programming in C++ requires a basic grasp of constructors, destructors, and inheritance— all of which depend on each other. Producing software that is both robust and of great quality also depends on this knowledge.

Advanced OOP Concepts

Considered by many as one of the most potent paradigms in the C++ programming language is object-oriented programming, or OOP. Advanced object-oriented programming concepts take modelling to the next level, even if basic ideas like classes, objects, encapsulation, inheritance, and polymorphism set the groundwork for knowing how to replicate software after real-world systems. By means of these advanced themes, developers can add a higher degree of sophistication to the ways in which they can structure, extend, and abstract their software architectures to generate codebases that are flexible, reusable, and easy to maintain over the years. Because of its great support of advanced object-oriented programming (OOP) capabilities, C++ distinguishes among programming languages. These features comprise abstract classes, interfaces, multiple inheritance, virtual functions and polymorphism, templates applied in concert with OOP ideas, operator overloading, and runtime type identification. Should developers be able to become experts in these disciplines, they would be able to create complex projects with improved scalability and performance whilst maintaining organization and clarity.

Among the most important advanced ideas in the object-oriented programming language C++ is abstraction enabled by abstract classes. An abstract class serves as a template for various different kinds of classes. It is meant to be inherited by classes derived from it, so instantiation of it is not possible on its own. Abstract classes differ from others in at least one pure virtual function inclusion. A pure virtual function is one described in the base class but lacking an implementation. Derived classes are hence required to satisfy this need and offer specific implementations for these pure virtual functions. Any class that derives from the abstract base must carry out the behaviours this design pattern suggests. This architectural form imposes a contract. Abstract classes have the power in their capacity to provide a shared interface for several related classes. This function allows certain implementation details to vary from one subclass to another while also making it possible to treat various objects in the same way. Large-scale systems' design often takes advantage of abstract classes. This is so even if numerous classes could exhibit identical behaviours but apply those characteristics in different combinations.

Interface use is based on abstraction and is a notion. Although C++ lacks a built-in "interface" keyword as some other languages do, it is nevertheless feasible to replicate interfaces using abstract classes, including just pure virtual functions and no data members. This approach is usually accepted since the C++ programming language is widely used to specify requirements that different classes are expected to comply with. Especially useful in the process of developing levels of abstraction in software, interfaces are used in cases when several components interact with one another under well defined contracts instead of through actual implementations. The development of code for interfaces instead of implementations allows developers more freedom and reduces the degree of component coupling. For the building of extensible systems, this is an absolutely vital quality.

Under deeper examination, another basic element of advanced object-oriented programming— polymorphism— showcases an even greater degree of usefulness. Polymorphism allows one to manage items of many kinds as though they were objects of a shared supertype. Virtual functions are the main way that polymorphism is achieved in C++. This approach lets derived classes overrule a function in a base class by designating it as virtual. When a virtual function is called upon when a base class pointer or reference is used to refer to an object of a derived class, the call is directed to the relevant derived class implementation to be run through at runtime. Apart from the basis of runtime polymorphism, this approach— known as dynamic dispatch— makes it feasible to create extremely flexible and adaptable code. This makes feasible techniques, including plugin structures, strategy patterns, and other polymorphic behaviours. These methods enable the precise type of the object to be chosen during running instead of at the moment of programming compilation.

Among object-oriented programming languages, one of the most remarkable features is the multiple inheritance support offered by C++. This function generates possible problems such as ambiguity and the diamond problem even though it offers significant capabilities for modelling real-world events and reusing code. When two or more base classes provide definitions for the same function or data member, a situation is left in flux. This causes the derived class to be unable to decide which version of the definition should be used. The diamond conundrum arises from a situation whereby a class inherits from two classes that inherit from a shared basis. Under such circumstances, the compiler may incorporate several copies of the shared base class into the inheritance structure, hence producing duplicated data and inconsistencies. Virtual inheritance is one way that C++ addresses these issues. This method marks base classes as virtual to ensure that, even in cases when there are many pathways to them, just one shared instance of the base class is inherited. Although it is a useful tool, multiple inheritances should be used carefully, and only once a thorough awareness of the consequences has been acquired.

Operator overloading is a further complex object-oriented programming concept that increases C++ code expressiveness. Thanks to operator overloading, developers can design their own unique behaviour for operators, including plus, minus, equal, and equal for user-defined types. This feature is particularly useful for developing classes that reflect mathematical abstractions like vectors, matrices, complex numbers, or complicated data structures since it lets one create such kinds of classes. Overloading operators helps developers create their classes more intuitive and user-friendly. This helps them to match the behaviour of their classes with those of built-in forms. Still, operator overloading should be used sensibly to prevent ambiguity and maintain the code's understandable nature. It is absolutely essential that it be always carried out in a way that preserves the intended semantics of the operator overloaded.

Templates in C++ present a strong method for reaching general programming. Combining this approach with object-oriented design produces incredibly type-safe and reusable code. Generic types only arise when a function is executed, or an instance is generated. Templates enable classes and operations to deal with general types. By using this capability, developers can create flexible code that runs with any data type without sacrificing type safety. Combining templates with inheritance and polymorphism allows one to produce increasingly sophisticated design patterns. Among these trends are type characteristics and policy-based design. For a data structure, for instance, an interface can be established using a class template. From there, some kinds can be entered as needed, which finally produces quite flexible implementations whilst still preserving consistency. Templates allow to elimination of duplicity and build strong type guarantees throughout the compilation process, which finally produces durable and easily maintained codebases.

Runtime Type Identification (RTTI), another complex concept in C++ Object-Oriented Programming (OOP), lets a program find the type of an object as it is being run. Situations involving polymorphism— more especially, those in which a base class reference might truly correspond to an object of a derived class— are most likely to call for RTTI. By means of the typeid operator and dynamic_cast, developers can securely investigate the type of an object and execute down casting when it is appropriate. Dynamic_cast is extremely helpful when dealing with big class hierarchies where safe type conversions are needed since it can convert several types. On the other hand, the use of RTTI has to be handled carefully since a too strong dependence on type checking during runtime could be suggestive of some design flaws.

Well-made polymorphic systems should, ideally, minimize the need for explicit type checks by depending on virtual functions and polymorphic behaviour.

Still another sophisticated capability present in C++ object-oriented programming is using friend classes and methods. By means of the buddy keyword, a non-member function or another class gains access to the members of a class currently under protection and privacy. Although this breaks the encapsulation barrier, occasionally, performance optimization or classes tightly coupled and need close access to each other's internals depend on this. Operator overloading is one of the most common application situations in input and output procedures. This happens when outside operations call for access to class internals. Though they can be quite successful, friend declarations should be used carefully to avoid compromising encapsulation and maintainability.

Delegation is another powerful object-oriented programming tool used often in advanced C++ designs. Sometimes, people refer to the act of one object depending on another helpful object to carry out a task as delegation. Delegation makes use of composition, which is when one object contains another object and assigns some responsibilities to what the other object is responsible for, rather than inheritance, in which case a subclass expands the capability of a superclass. This approach gives more flexibility and promotes the reusing of code since it removes the strict coupling resulting from inheritance. Delegation makes dynamic assignment of behaviour at runtime feasible; it is a necessary component of many different design patterns, including the decorator pattern and the strategy pattern.

Though they are not unique to C++, the SOLID ideas provide the basis of well-structured object-oriented design that is growing crucial in advanced programming. Following these guidelines helps you to guarantee that classes are orderly, that duties are clearly defined, and that the system is easy to run and expand from. For instance, the Open/Closed Principle supports classes to be open for expansion but closed for modification. This method fits the use of virtual functions and polymorphism rather perfectly. Following these ideas helps developers to design simpler to test and debug systems as well as scalable, trustworthy solutions.

Furthermore, especially in more complicated systems, memory management in C++ is intimately related to object-oriented techniques. Unlike languages that allow garbage collecting that occur automatically, memory management in C++ must be done explicitly. Advanced C++ programmers must use great care when handling dynamic memory allocation and deallocation to prevent issues such as segmentation errors, dangling pointers, and memory leaks. Originally presented in the C++ Standard Library, smart pointers offer a modern method by automating memory management via reference counting and scope-bound resource management. Safe and effective memory management can be obtained by combining smart pointers such as unique_ptr, shared_ptr, and weak_ptr with classes and objects. This then improves the general resilience of C++ systems grounded on object-oriented programming.

Furthermore, included in advanced object-oriented programming in the C++ programming language are design pattern implementation and application. Reusable solutions available for many different software design problems are design patterns. The computer language C++ makes regular use of patterns, including Singleton, Factory, Abstract Factory, Observer, and Visitor, in order to handle architectural concerns. These trends help to capture best practices and offer solutions based on proven success for organizing things and classrooms. For example, the Factory Pattern is widely used to capture object manufacturing, therefore simplifying the modification of the logic of instantiation without requiring rewriting of the client code. Furthermore, often used in event-driven systems for the aim of creating a one-to-many relationship between objects is the Observer Pattern. This relationship helps one item undergo modifications that are conveyed to other objects.

Following the concept of separation of concerns becomes ever more important while handling major projects. Regarding sophisticated object-oriented programming in C++, there is often a need to separate class responsibilities and control dependencies via interfaces and abstractions. Dependency injection is more prevalent in languages that have built-in support for reflection, but it is still feasible in C++ by using factory methods and explicitly providing dependencies. Reducing the degree of reliance between classes and supporting the use of mock objects during unit testing helps this approach increase testability and maintainability.

In essence, sophisticated object-oriented programming methods in C++ provide developers with a strong toolkit that helps them to create smart, flexible, and efficient software systems. Apart from abstract classes and polymorphism, C++ lets run-through type identification, multiple inheritance, and templates. These qualities enable the programming language to faithfully and maintainably represent complex systems. Proper knowledge of these ideas and applications will help one to attain better code design, more code reuse, and lower maintenance expenses. If developers have perfected advanced object-oriented programming techniques, they can create systems that are not just strong and high-performance but also scalable and resilient in the face of evolving needs.

CHAPTER VII

File Handling, Error Handling, and Final Project

File Handling in C++

File handling offers a way to read from and write to persistent storage, unlike dealing just with memory whilst a program is running. This guarantees that information can be kept long after the application has been closed. From simple programs tracking user activity to more sophisticated systems, including databases, media players, or any other tool requiring permanent data, a wide spectrum of software must have this capability. Designing reasonable, real-world applications that manage data in a fast and safe way depends on a strong knowledge of how the C++ file handling system works.

File handling management in C++ is accomplished via a standard library known as <fstream>. Several useful courses provided by this library can be applied for file input and output operations processing. Inherited and expanded from the C standard library, the stream-based input/output system in C++ was improved with object-oriented concepts. The greater stream-based I/O system consists of these classes. The process of file processing entails three main types of classes. These classes are ifstream, which manages input file streams, ofstream, which manages output file streams; and fstream, which manages both input and output employing the same file. These classes provide a user interface that anyone who has worked with basic console input/output in C++ will be familiar with since they are meant to imitate the capability of the cin and cout commands.

Usually, starting with opening a file using one of the file stream classes, working with files follows this sequence. Depending on the action that is being done, files can be opened read-only, write-only, append, or any mix of reading and writing. One can indicate these modes by using preset flags. Among these flags are ios ::in, ios ::out, and ios ::app. Combining these settings using the bitwise OR operator allows one to open files in many modes concurrently. Not opening a file in the proper way is rather crucial since neglect to do so could cause software crashes, data loss, or other unanticipated events. Make sure the file has been opened successfully with suitable permissions before moving on with activities on a file. Usually, this is achieved by using built-in member functions or by analysing the state of the file stream under a conditional expression.

Reading data from a file can be managed in several ways inside the C++ framework, depending on the structure and format of the data. In dealing with structured data in which every line or token has a predefined meaning, the extraction operator— which is similar to the cin operator— is used often. This method allows the program to smoothly read and write data into variables of a great range of kinds. Functions like getline() allow one to execute more flexible reading, that is, reading a whole line or a block of text. When working with natural language text or papers that have been structured, this approach— which scans a whole line of text, including spaces— is really useful. When binary files are involved, one must use more advanced reading techniques. Among these techniques include the use of read functions designed for raw byte data handling. These let the application read the contents of the file in line with a binary format unique to it. Image processing, audio encoding, and game development all depend on this ability quite a bit.

Writing to a file requires first producing an output file stream and then using the insertion operator— akin to the cout command— to move data to the file. Depending on the needs of the application, data can be entered in either binary or text form. Regarding text-based files, formatting is easy, and the output features give a lot of control over the way the data is displayed. Newlines, tabs, and even format strings and numbers can all be included by developers in a variety of ways. Raw byte storage in binary files is a common use for the write() function among programmers. This feature ensures that, upon file reading back at a later period, the data structure will stay unaltered. One must have a more in-depth knowledge of the way data is kept in memory, including issues with byte order, padding, and alignment, therefore enabling proper management of binary data.

In C++, one of the most important parts of file handling is the proper management of resources. This entails not only whether or not a file has been opened successfully but also ensuring that the file closes once the corresponding activities have been completed. It is advised to explicitly stop files by using the close() function, even though C++ destructors will automatically terminate file streams when objects leave their scope. This guarantees instant file handle relinquishment and writes to disk of any buffered data. This is especially important for initiatives involving a lot of files or long-running operations across several departments. Particularly in cases where the application crashes or is halted suddenly before the operating system has flushed all buffers, the failure to close files might cause data corruption.

Another fundamental component of the file input and output process is handling mistakes. Working with files could cause files not existing, insufficient permissions, disk full errors, or corrupted file contents, among other issues. One can find these issues challenging. The features C++ offers help one to discover and manage these issues elegantly. File stream classes incorporate a number of member methods, including fail(), eof(), bad(), and good(). The several states of the stream are found by use of these operations. These features let one ascertain whether an error has occurred, whether the file's finish has been reached, or whether the stream is still in an acceptable condition. If developers check these criteria before starting file operations, they can stop unanticipated behaviour and give the user helpful comments.

Advanced file handling methods in C++ call for manipulation of file references. File pointers establish the location inside the file from which data is read or to which data is written. Functions like seekg() for input streams and seekp() for output streams let one move the pointers to files about. These methods allow for random file contents access. The internal pointer is moved in line with the offset position and the direction— beginning, current, or end of the file— that these operations offer. This feature is particularly useful for building bespoke file-based data structures like databases or indexed logs or when handling large files since it facilitates more effective file manipulation. Having the option to go straight to a specific file section without reading over the whole contents helps both performance and efficiency.

Binary file management is the more specialized domain of C++ file I/O. This domain is often used in circumstances when data integrity and compactness are absolutely critical. Unlike text files, which humans can read, binary files contain data in a format that lets the machine use it straightforwardly. This shows that the raw memory form of data structures may be written and read, therefore facilitating faster and more effective data access. Conversely, binary files are not without extra challenges. Troubleshooting them could be difficult for the basic reason humans cannot understand them. Furthermore, influencing the portability of binary files are variations in endianness, structural padding, and data type sizes across systems. To ensure compatibility with forward and backward versions of the file, it is thus essential to pay considerable care to the way data is written and read and include metadata or versioning information into the file format.

These formats are text-based; hence, some parsing and formatting standards become essential, even if their comprehension depends on other factors. For example, rows and columns make up comma-separated values (CSV) files, whereby a comma separates every value. Reading these kinds of files requires more than just reading a line; one must also dissect that line down into its component elements. JSON and XML demand considerably more complicated processing because of their hierarchical structure and nesting possibilities, which usually call for the employment of specific libraries. Third-party libraries like RapidJSON and TinyXML are routinely used in spite of the fact that the standard library of C++ does not include native support for JSON or XML processing to achieve these chores. Including such libraries in a C++ application shows how file handling covers more general issues, including structural interpretation, data serialization, and format validation. This transcends the basic reading and writing activities usually connected with file processing.

File handling in C++ applications used in the real world sometimes crosses with the management of configurations and user interactions. For example, programs might preserve local application user preferences or system configurations in files. This file has to be accessed at the start of the procedure and might change while the application is in operation. Strong file handlers are needed to ensure that such data is kept consistently and does not vanish between sessions. Creating log files— which applications employ to document events, problems, or transaction data for later analysis— is another often utilized use for them. Under these kinds of circumstances, the ability to append to files without rewriting the already existing data becomes really crucial. Essential also is the ability to rotate and archive logs when they grow too big.

System programming and running operating-system programs depend critically on the way files are handled as well. File descriptors and low-level file operations are thus involved in these activities. Sometimes, especially in hardware-specific or performance-critical scenarios, it is especially crucial to interface directly with system calls or lower-level APIs. While C++'s standard file stream classes help to abstract a good amount of these low-level functionalities, occasionally, direct communication is needed. Developers may use the C-style fopen, fread, fwrite, and fclose features for file mapping, asynchronous input and output, and device file access— or even the operating system's offered application programming interfaces (APIs).

Multiple threads and concurrent access to files add still another level of complexity to file processing. When several threads or processes can access the same file, synchronizing is necessary. This helps to stop data races and inconsistent behaviour. File locking and mutexes help one to guarantee that only one thread is writing to a file at any one point and to limit access as well. File handling in distributed systems can refer to cloud-based storage or network file systems, both of which are further considerations along with latency and data consistency. Though these components are beyond the capacity of conventional C++, the basic ideas of file management remain applicable and are the basis upon which such sophisticated systems are built.

Learning file handling in the programming language C++ in educational situations often marks a student's development from basic, isolated programs to more complex, stateful applications. Exercises including reading data from files, analysing that data, and giving the results back to disk can teach one how to work with persistent data. These drills give essential experience. These activities also highlight the need for user input, data validation, and software resilience, therefore strengthening another aspect. Students begin to see trends in file management and design elements that can be used again as they progress in their studies, therefore streamlining the process. Whether it's the building blocks for more complex programming jobs— configuration parsers, save/load mechanisms for games, or tools to process log files— the skills gained via knowledge of file handling support each other.

In software development, C++ file handling is a fundamental competency that forms the basis of a great range of jobs. Programs can retain data over several program runs by closing the gap between transient memory operations and long-term data storage. From simple tasks like reading a list of names to more complex operations involving binary file formats and structured data parsing, a wide spectrum of jobs depends on the capacity to manage files. Because of the strength and adaptability C++ provides in this field, developers can design scalable and effective applications. Object-oriented architecture, stream-based input and output, and low-level system access C++ provide help to make this feasible. Proficient file processing helps developers create not only functional but also strong, user-friendly, and capable of significant interactions with the world outside the immediate runtime environment applications.

Error Handling and Debugging

Two of the most important components of software development are the way mistakes are handled and the debugging process. These elements define the basis of reliable, strong, and straightforward to administer application. Some aspects of programming really set novice programmers apart from more experienced ones. These features consist of the careful control of mistakes and the thorough debugging procedure. One of the most often held false ideas about programming is that creating code is a fascinating aspect of the process. This isn't the case, though. These strategies are especially helpful in the framework of learning C++ since the language gives a great degree of control over resources at the system level. On the other side, if this is not managed properly, this creates the risk of producing minor but significant mistakes. Such mistakes may have grave results. Beginning users should especially pay close attention to have a strong awareness of how to foresee, recognize, and handle issues as they advance from developing simple programs to building more complicated applications. This has to be done if we are to ensure that mistakes are not missed.

When it comes to programming, mistakes are inevitable. The experience level of a developer has no bearing on their probability of making mistakes. These challenges can show up as runtime mistakes, syntactic errors, and logical errors as well as more general ones. Usually, the least complicated aspect of the correction process is the one involving grammar mistakes. This is so because the compiler can pretty consistently spot syntactic mistakes. For example, any semicolons lacking, erroneous variable declarations, or misplaced parenthesis are quickly identified and recorded throughout the compilation process. This maintains the code's integrity. Conversely, when it comes to spotting runtime and logical mistakes, the compiler is less efficient than when it comes to spotting syntax mistakes. Runtime errors are those that develop naturally during the running of a program. These mistakes could arise from improper behaviour, including accessing objects of an array outside of their boundaries, dividing by zero, or dereferencing null pointers at the same time. From a technical standpoint, however, logical mistakes usually prove the most difficult to spot and fix. These mistakes arise when the program runs without breaking but generates insufficient output instead of what is required. This is the outcome of the faulty logic applied by the developer.

The computer language C++ provides a range of choices among the several ways one can control and solve mistakes. One of the most important weapons in this regard is the capacity to foretell issues and treat them in a way that is both orderly and polite. Among the tools thought to be most crucial are those related to exception management. Writing, reading, and changing the code is much simplified by isolating the main logic of the application from the error-handy code using exceptions. In computer language C++, an exception is regarded to be thrown upon unanticipated events. The element in charge of managing mistakes is then the catch block, which the control is shifted to. The management of unavoidable mistakes— such as failures in file I/O, memory allocation issues, or user incorrect input— that cannot be prevented makes especially great use of this approach. This approach is really helpful since it lets one control these mistakes by means of management. Anyone who wants to be competent in the management of mistakes in the C++ programming language has to be able to make efficient use of exceptions.

Still, exceptions are not necessary to manage all C++ errors, nor should they be applied to all situations. Not should they be applied to every issue as well. Many times, it is feasible to prevent exceptions on purpose while handling performance-critical codes. This is very common while working on codes. Developers typically rely on error codes, assertions, or whole customized error-handling systems whenever something like this occurs place. Though this strategy calls for more human management, it provides more exact control over the way problems are found and addressed. Those who are just starting their professions should give getting a thorough awareness of the situation under which it is acceptable to employ exceptions and the circumstances under which an alternative strategy would be more appropriate top importance. One could only have this realization by means of experience as well as a more in-depth awareness of the design and performance requirements of the application.

Debugging helps to control errors by helping developers find and fix the flaws causing these problems. Debugging is a thorough method used in detecting, isolating, and fixing problems in the code that call for all three actions. Being both an art and a science, one must have throughout the process patience, critical thinking, and meticulous attention to detail. Usually starting with the reproduction of the issue, the debugging process starts numerous times in the initial stage. Appreciating the issue and coming up with a fix becomes somewhat challenging when a glitch cannot be consistently replicated. The developers will be able to start evaluating the flow of the program as well as the condition of its variables at the point where the program fails once they have proved that the error can be generated in a consistent manner.

Regarding debugging, one of the most basic strategies that has shown to be quite helpful is using print statements. Incorporating comments showing varying values and execution progress helps developers see what the program is doing and where it might be failing. Variables and execution progress show here that this is possible. Moreover, even if this approach is straightforward, it could be rather helpful especially in initiatives less complex or in situations when more potent debugging tools are not accessible. Conversely, as software size and complexity keep rising, demand for ever more advanced debugging tools is rising as well.

Modern integrated development environments (IDEs) provide strong debugging tools built-in without further installation required. These tools have breakpoint settings, step through code line by line, variable value inspection, and even memory data modification capability while the program is running. Thanks to these tools, developers can access all of these features. Because they let developers stop the program's running at certain lines of code, breakpoints are quite helpful for them. This lets them look at the state of the application under that specific situation. Developers particularly benefit from breakpoints. Considering this data helps one to better grasp the underlying cause of a program behaving in an unexpected way. Step execution makes it considerably easier for the developer to spot logical errors or unanticipated branching in the control flow since it helps them see the reasoning of the program in action. This is so because step execution enables the developer to see the program's logic in operation.

Apart from the traditional debugging instruments already in use, developers could also take advantage of more sophisticated techniques such as memory profilers, static analysis tools, and logging systems. These are only a handful of the kind of approaches developers could use. A useful tool for finding memory leaks and examples of inefficiently used memory is the memory profiler. In the computer language C++, where memory management is typically done manually, this is of the most relevance. Static analysis tools help to examine code without actually running it in order to find possible flaws that can develop. These instruments can spot issues, including type incompatibilities between variables, code inaccessible, or variables not initializing themselves. Thanks to logging systems that enable this feature, it is possible to document occurrences occurring during the running of a program. This is a very useful skill when it comes to solving issues that only surface seldom or in production environments where direct debugging is forbidden.

Having a strong awareness of the variations between symptoms and the elements generating them is also absolutely important for the debugging process. Sometimes beginners try to fix symptoms, meaning they change code in a way that suggests the problem will be resolved without looking at the root cause of the problem. One typical error beginner make is this one. Moreover, this can result in behaviour going forward that is erratic or unanticipated. A deeper exploration of the logic and structure of the program is necessary for good debugging to help one grasp the causes of the problem and the ways in which it might be avoided from the starting point. This is essential to guarantee correct debugging of the software. To reach this aim, one could have to investigate the design of the program, investigate the presumptions put into the code, and evaluate edge scenarios that might not have been first considered.

Furthermore, crucial are good coding practices so that debugging and error control are executed effectively. It is much easier to find and fix mistakes in a clean, well-organized piece of code with consistent names that are understandable, sufficient indentation, and suitable comments. Functionality in modular design is divided down into smaller, more controllable components, which helps to isolate issues and directs troubleshooting. Moreover, modular architecture facilitates the solution of challenges. Another very useful tool for both software debugging and error prevention is the application of unit testing. By means of the construction of tests that assess the validity of specific functions or modules, developers can find mistakes at an earlier stage in the development process. This helps developers make sure changes do not bring about fresh flaws.

Debugging is usually part of a team effort among several persons in settings dedicated to professional growth. Code reviews are a typical activity when colleagues check the code of one another to find possible problems. This guarantees that appropriate coding standards are followed for the length of the project and guarantees the information flow, helping to identify mistakes that the original developer could have missed. Pair programming, a type of software development whereby two developers work together at the same workstation, can also be useful for identifying and repairing problems since it combines two different sets of eyes and ideas to solve an issue.

One cannot stress the need for documentation all through the error-handling and debugging process. One cannot exaggerate its importance. Good documentation helps one to understand how a piece of code is anticipated to operate and also facilitates the identification of areas in which things do not go as expected. This is so that one may better understand how things ought to be run. Included here are outside world documentation like design documents, use guidelines, and problem reports. This covers not only remarks on the code but also outside world documentation. Writing bug reports that are not only very clear but also rather particular helps one to monitor the fixing of discovered flaws. Furthermore, it offers a background that could come in handy should similar kinds of problems develop going forward.

Technical knowledge alone will not help you be successful in error handling and debugging; you also need the correct mindset. Approaching problems with curiosity and resolve instead of frustration is a more effective way to solve them than in a frustrated manner. Insects should be seen as chances to learn more about the system and enhance the developed code rather than as failures. As time goes on and developers get more expertise, they start to become aware of where issues are likely to show up and how best to approach effective debugging of them. As one learns more, this awareness begins to change.

Two abilities absolutely required of a coder in their toolset are error management and debugging. For those who are currently learning a language like C++, this is particularly true. One must have a great awareness of the several kinds of faults, be competent in the tools and procedures for seeing and fixing problems, and follow high coding standards if one wants to create reliable, straightforward, maintainable software. These constitute the requirements that have to be satisfied. These features not only raise the general calibre of the programs but also help the author to find the process of production more controllable and rewarding. If beginning programmers see error handling and debugging as fundamental elements of the development process, they will be more ready to manage progressively challenging jobs with confidence and competency as they travel through their adventure with C++.

Final Project - A Mini C++ Application

For a rookie starting their journey into the realm of programming, the beginning of the process of building a small C++ application as a final project marks a turning point. This effort not only helps to consolidate the acquired theoretical knowledge from studies but also offers real-world experience in the planning, development, and management of a software project from the start to the finish. Among the several tasks needed before the process can be deemed finished are brainstorming, planning, coding, testing, and documentation. Completing each of these stages will help one to acquire a thorough awareness of software development approaches.

The first phase of the process is choosing a project idea that fits the developer's interests and current degree of expertise. This helps the developer to decide with knowledge. Selecting a project that is not only interesting but also sufficiently demanding is essential since it will guarantee that one is motivated for a significant period of time and will provide chances for very valuable learning opportunities. Projects usually advocated for novices are a banking system, a tic-tac-toe game, or a student management system. Other instances include gaming systems. These projects present a reasonable challenge, and they give chances to use basic programming concepts. We do suggest that you do these projects. For example, a project involving a banking system allows one to explore file handling operations and switch-case statements, therefore offering a useful background for the ideas under discussion.

Once the project's concept has been decided upon, one must proceed with painstaking planning to explain the features, functionalities, and general architecture of the program. The concept of the project comes next, determined. At this level, you will be in charge of several tasks like project core component selection, development timetable creation, and project goal defining. Making thorough flow charts and diagrams will help one visualize the structure and behaviour of the system, therefore facilitating the eventual more effective implementation process. Since they are thorough, flow charts and diagrams can be produced. Furthermore, considering prospective issues and developing plans to handle them ahead of time helps one to reduce the degree of difficulty encountered during the process of development.

Theoretical knowledge is turned into useful application during the coding process, therefore enabling its implementation. The use of an integrated development environment (IDE) might be able to increase productivity degree. This is thus since the IDE offers tools for testing, debugging, and code development. Following best practices helps one to improve the maintainability and readability of the program by means of modular code, uniform naming standards, and clear integration of comments. These all represent best practices. Thus, it is imperative to incorporate error handling techniques in order to ensure that the program is able to elegantly manage unexpected inputs or situations, which will finally result in an increase in its resilience. This will finally help the program to resist unanticipated circumstances to be better.

An essential part of the development process, the testing stage seeks to find and resolve any possible flaws or problems inside the program. This ensures that the parts are operating as they should. Usually including iterative cycles of testing and debugging, this phase calls for both patience and meticulous attention to detail. This phase also regularly calls for close attention to those specifics. Effective debugging techniques, including using print statements or applying debugging tools provided by the integrated development environment (IDE), can help to identify the cause of problems and simplify their fixing.

Though it is a necessary component of the software development process, documentation is often neglected even if it is quite important. Using thorough documentation allows one to have an understanding of the program's design, functionality, and application. For future maintenance or for other developers who may be working on the project, this material is a great tool to use. Apart from providing detailed references on the architecture and data flow of the program, this feature also covers the development of user manuals, the analysis of intricate code sections, and the distribution of those precise details. Thorough documentation of projects not only shows professionalism but also helps the program to be scalable and durable.

Should the project be finished, it would be advisable to spend some time considering the development process and the difficulties that were satisfactorily resolved. This offers an opportunity for both intellectual development and personal improvement. Reviewing which tactics worked well and pointing up areas that might use development will help one develop problem-solving abilities and guide the next tasks. This assessment helps to guide the next projects by means of direction. Furthermore, asking for the opinions of mentors or peers will provide fresh ideas and viewpoints that support the development of both personally and professionally.

I would want to say that the process of finishing a final project involving the building of a small C++ application using the language catches the essence of learning by doing. Doing this helps to close the gap between theoretical knowledge and the actual application of such information, therefore promoting the growth of a deeper awareness of technical programming principles and software development methods. The result of this effort is not only the production of a physical good but also provides a strong basis for the next programming projects.

CONCLUSION

Completing C++ for Beginners: Your First Programming Language Explained - Understand Core C++ Concepts with Practical Examples is reason for celebration! By now, you have a good grasp of the fundamental ideas connected to C++. Together with fundamental grammar and data types, these ideas include object-oriented programming, memory management, and file handling. Furthermore, you have worked on a final project and gone through particular cases, so you are gaining real world knowledge in creating actual C++ programs.

Learning C++ is an interesting trip you are about to start. Constant experimentation, the building of projects, and the search for fresh problems ought to be kept in progress. As you keep learning, you can develop an interest in more difficult topics, including algorithms, data structures, and game development. All these subjects draw on the basic ideas covered in C++ for Beginners.

Should you choose to be a professional software developer, create your own projects, or just learn how programming works, you now have the means to boldly move forward with your next activities. You have just begun your journey across the vast and rich world of C++.

Always acquire new skills, keep coding, and enjoy the process. Programming has to be enjoyable!

Thank you for buying and reading/ listening to our book. If you found this book useful/ helpful please take a few minutes and leave a review on the platform where you purchased our book. Your feedback matters greatly to us.

www.ingramcontent.com/pod-product-compliance
Lightning Source LLC
LaVergne TN
LVHW022100200926
848481LV00003B/1012